RAISING EMOTIONAL INTELLIGENCE

RAY LAFERLA

Other Books by Ray Laferla:
The Leading Edge in Management
Discover Your Management Style
Discover Your Psychological Type
The Freedom of Forgiveness
Empowered Living
Enabled to Grow
Mastering Emotional Intelligence

Published by Integrated Human Dynamics, Johannesburg, South Africa
Email: rlaferla@ihdynamics.co.za
www.ihdynamics.co.za

TABLE OF CONTENTS

PREFACE

Emotional Intelligence is a concept that Peter Salovey, a professor at Yale University, and John Mayer, a postdoctoral researcher, first identified in 1990. Psychologist Daniel Goleman later popularised it in his book "Emotional Intelligence", published in 1995.

As the term implies, Emotional Intelligence has to do with the effective use of emotions, whether it emanates from oneself or others. People with high Emotional Intelligence understand that humans are emotional beings and that emotions must be managed and regulated to build relationships and achieve goals.

Before the idea of Emotional Intelligence was introduced, psychologists thought intelligence was innate and could be revealed by administering a series of standardised tests called IQ Tests. (IQ stands for Intelligence Quotient) The implication was that people with a high IQ were intellectually superior to those with an average IQ.

Salovey, Mayer, and Goleman questioned this hypothesis because they noticed that people with a high IQ were often less successful than those with an average IQ. High-IQ individuals performed better academically but could not always apply their Intelligence to other aspects of life, especially relationships, including teamwork.

Enter Emotional Intelligence (EQ). Further research revealed that a person with an average IQ and a high EQ did better than someone with a high IQ and a low EQ. There are reasons for this phenomenon. IQ is a logical-mathematical construct that uses logical reasoning to understand the world and come to conclusions. However, we are seldom motivated by reason alone. We often make decisions based on feelings and are frequently moved by unconscious urges driven by our emotions.

Because IQ and Emotional Intelligence (EQ) represent opposite traits, someone with a high IQ is likely to be deficient in understanding people who value feelings more than logic. These individuals may have difficulty regulating their emotions to build effective relationships. Albert Einstein is a good example of this.

In 1952, Israel's first president, Chaim Weizman, died. Because Einstein was a genius and regarded as "the greatest Jew alive", he was invited to be the nation's second president. Einstein turned down the offer saying, *"All my life, I have dealt with objective matters, hence I lack both the natural aptitude and the experience to deal properly with people and to exercise official functions"*.

Even though the concept of Emotional Intelligence did not exist at the time, Einstein knew that he did not have the people skills to comprehend the motivations of others and make decisions to serve the citizens of Israel. Consequently, he did not see himself as being a good president.

We see, then, that IQ and EQ are different types of intelligences, each having particular strengths and weaknesses. IQ is important for rational decision-making, strategic thinking, and data analysis. However, it does not deal adequately with subjective factors such as happiness, social skills, intuition and feelings. EQ, on the other hand, is more important for getting along and connecting with others. It is an interpersonal intelligence that relates to social skills such as empathy, non-judgment, collaboration and communication. These domains are largely subjective, which is why IQ often struggles with them.

Since people will naturally have a dominant IQ or EQ, is it possible to raise whichever is wanting? The answer to this question is yes. However, IQ is more difficult to improve as it is a cognitive function that depends primarily on education and genetic factors.

EQ, however, is a much more amenable trait that can be raised by becoming aware of how feelings drive behaviour and acquiring a range of personal and interpersonal skills such as listening, self-discipline, resilience and empathy. In addition, coaches, teachers, people and counsellors can help people improve coping and relational skills.

Since research has found that EQ is a good predictor of success and happiness in life, it behoves us to increase our knowledge and application of Emotional Intelligence as much as possible to raise EQ.

The reason I have written this book is, therefore, to provide information describing the nature and domains of Emotional Intelligence, and offer specific tools and strategies for developing key skills in those domains.

The four domains of EQ are:

- Self-Awareness,
- Self-Management,
- Social-Awareness, and
- Relationship Management.

By reading this book and implementing the strategies given, both individuals and facilitators of personal growth (such as coaches, teachers, people and counsellors) will know how to:

- Identify and label emotions accurately;
- Express feelings in ways that enhance relationships and achieve desired outcomes;
- Understand others and empathise with them;
- Practice rational thinking to manage emotions;
- Forgive self and others to mitigate the burden of holding on to the pain of the past;
- Manage conflict;
- Practice self-discipline;
- Build good habits;
- Be an effective listener;
- Create trust;
- Influence and persuade others;
- Deal with difficult people.

After introducing readers to EQ's meaning, domains and importance, each chapter will cover a specific skill and offer tools and strategies for raising Emotional Intelligence. Readers will also find practical examples and stories that clarify concepts and illustrate how tactics are applied in real life.

By familiarising yourself with the contents of this book and applying the techniques given, you will be able to transform your life. If you facilitate the growth of others, you will know what actions to take to make a difference in the lives of those you influence. Overall, you will discover opportunities and know-how to unlock potential and raise the Emotional Intelligence of yourself and others for the benefit of everyone.

Ray Laferla

RAISING EMOTIONAL INTELLIGENCE

Understanding Emotional Intelligence (EQ)

Ray Laferla

1: THE MEANING, DOMAINS, AND IMPORTANCE OF EMOTIONAL INTELLIGENCE

What Is Emotional Intelligence?

Emotions drive most of our behaviours, no matter how logical or rational we think we are. Emotions are also the filters through which we perceive and understand the world, including people's motives and events.

Emotional Intelligence embraces skills that describe how effectively we recognise, understand, use, and manage our own, and others, feelings. It also embodies how well we relate and engage with others, personally and professionally.

Emotional Intelligence is often denoted by the symbols EQ (Emotional Quotient) or EI (Emotional Intelligence). The most commonly used of these two is EQ because it is often compared with IQ (Intelligence Quotient), which is a logical-mathematical construct.

How do we identify a person with a high EQ? What behaviours would we observe? Emotional intelligent people:

- Are good at acknowledging and managing their emotions. They are aware of the nature of their feelings (they can name them), know where they come from and can express them appropriately. Emotionally intelligent people do not let their emotions overwhelm them, they can exercise, control and direct their feelings, no matter how difficult or frustrating the situation is,
- Are comfortable with who they are. They are at ease showing compassion, empathy, and appreciation,
- Are in tune with themselves and the people around them.

They are neither sceptical nor naive, knowing when to trust others and when to be more careful,

- Are able to motivate themselves under all circumstances,
- Are caring and considerate, yet firm and resolute. They stand up for what they believe and do not compromise their values. When wrong, they are able to admit it and apologise,
- Are good communicators. In most circumstances, they have the sensitivity to express themselves appropriately. They are also trusted and find it easy to influence and persuade people. They never take advantage of others, manipulate people or act against their colleagues, subordinates, customers, or friends,
- Take time to reflect on their behaviours and are willing to look at themselves honestly. They take responsibility for their actions and don't shift blame onto others,
- Take setbacks in their stride and are optimistic. They inspire others to take a positive view of things and solve problems rather than dwell on negatives. And when they can't change anything, they accept the situation and move on without bitterness or resentment,
- Can get in touch with, and respond appropriately, to the emotional needs of people.

The Difference Between Feelings And Emotions

Most people use the terms 'feelings' and 'emotions' interchangeably, with little distinction between the two. There is, however, a difference.

A feeling is an internal sensation that is felt but may be hidden or suppressed. It is an inner sentiment that is unknown to others unless expressed. In other words, people will not see what you feel unless you tell or show them.

An emotion, on the other hand, is observed in behaviours and actions. Unlike feelings, others will see emotions in expressions and behaviours such as crying, sweating, facial expressions, body postures, etc.

The Domains And Competencies Of Emotional Intelligence

There are two categories of Emotional Intelligence, namely Personal and Interpersonal.

Within these categories, there are four domains, or skill groups, namely:

- Self-Awareness
- Self-Management ⎬ Personal Domains

- Social Awareness
- Relationship Management ⎬ Interpersonal Domains

Let us now examine the requisite skills under each competency.

Self-Awareness

Self-Awareness is *"The ability to recognise and name feelings, differentiate between them, and know what caused them."* It is the foundation that underscores all EQ competencies because we cannot understand and know what other people are feeling unless we recognise that feeling in ourselves.

Self-Awareness is knowing what occurs internally and what emotions drive our behaviours. The more self-aware we are, the better we are able to monitor and control our actions.

Without Self-Awareness, our emotions may cause us to overreact and behave irrationally, in ways that embitter and hurt, negatively impacting our relationships with others. We are also inclined to blame people, circumstances, and events for our problems, not accepting personal responsibility. Consequently, we are likely to repeat indiscretions and remain in bondage to external factors and undesirable circumstances.

When we become aware of our feelings, and what causes them, we can choose our responses to a given situation. Exercising this choice empowers us to take control of our behaviours and direct them towards satisfying and meaningful ends.

Self-Awareness embraces the following:

- Recognising and naming feelings;
- Understanding emotions;
- Using an "Emotional Scale" to determine dominant emotions;
- Appraising yourself on the fourteen qualities of emotionally intelligent people.

Self-Management

Self-Management is *"Regulating, managing and changing an inappropriate or dysfunctional emotional state."*

Whereas the first requirement of EQ is to know what we feel, and where these feelings come from, the second step is to regulate or manage them so that they benefit rather than harm us.

Our sentiments and emotions can energise and motivate actions, but they can also make us sad, discouraged and experience negative sensations. To counter this situation, we need to exercise Self-Management, which is another word for self-control.

Self-Management enables us to act with purpose and intention rather than reactively. The competencies in this domain empower us to change negative feelings to constructive ones. They embody practical tools to manage our moods and perceive events in ways that enable us to overcome problems with positive attitudes.

Seven strategies are employed to manage oneself:
- Implementing strategies for successful achievement;
- Using physiology to create empowering mental states;
- Applying self-discipline;
- Building resilience and mental toughness;
- Forming good habits and overcoming bad habits;
- Employing rational thinking to manage emotions;
- Engaging forgiveness to achieve emotional freedom.

Social-Awareness

Emotional Intelligence includes tuning in to the feelings of those we interact with. It means responding to others appropriately, with sensitivity and compassion.

An important factor in the interpersonal domain of EQ is to acknowledge other people's feelings and emotions – be they sad, happy, confused, angry or anything else, while keeping in mind that these emotions belong to them and are not ours. A certain amount of detachment is, therefore, necessary when dealing with the feelings of others.

In other words, we endeavour to understand why people behave the way they do, without taking responsibility for their words or actions, and engage with them appropriately.

Three critical elements of Social-Awareness are:
- Practising empathy;
- Being non-judgemental;
- Transmuting the emotions of others.

Relationship Management
The last EQ competency is about engaging with people to establish satisfying and productive relationships. To achieve this, we require the following skills:
- Influencing with integrity,
- Managing conflict,
- Dealing with difficult people.

The Importance Of Emotional Intelligence
Emotional Intelligence plays an essential role in achieving success for three reasons:

i. Successful achievement requires overcoming inherent negative attributes such as procrastination, negative emotions, lack of motivation, discouragement, and many others. Unless we know how to overcome these challenges, we will get stuck and fail to achieve our desires. This is why so few people are successful, with the vast majority living dull, mediocre and unfulfilling lives. Henry Thoreau expressed this by saying, "The mass of men lead lives of quiet desperation".

ii. People with high emotional intelligence know how to take charge of themselves and achieve a full, satisfying life. They do this by understanding themselves, managing their emotions, applying self-discipline and doing whatever it takes.

iii. No one can be successful without the support and cooperation of others. Furthermore, even if we did succeed on our own, we would find it meaningless.

Suppose you decided to climb a high mountain that is treacherous and difficult. You worked hard and eventually stood at the peak of the mountain, thinking you succeeded without the assistance of others. Is this true?

No, it's not. Why? Because hundreds of people enabled you to achieve your goal the designers and workers who manufactured the equipment you used, the mountaineers who went before you, providing you with knowledge of the terrain, people from whom you learnt the techniques of rock climbing, the availability of specialists if you run into difficulties, etc.;

Then, having succeeded in your quest, you stand at the top of the mountain and realise that you are all alone. There is no back-slapping, no whooping, and nobody with whom to share your accomplishment. Suddenly your joy seems hollow. It wasn't supposed to be like this. It was supposed to be a life-fulfilling accomplishment. What went wrong?

Only with people can we be truly successful. Nobody is independent; we are all interdependent, needing others to succeed and enjoy the fruits of our achievements. Jim Rohn said, *"You cannot succeed by yourself. It's hard to find a rich hermit."*

Emotionally intelligent people are aware that others are important in their lives. They, therefore, develop social and relationship skills that attract people, communicate with others, demonstrate compassion, are good listeners and engage a host of attributes that build relationships.

Ray Laferla

RAISING EMOTIONAL INTELLIGENCE

The First Domain of EQ: Self-Awareness

Ray Laferla

RAISING EMOTIONAL INTELLIGENCE

Self-Awareness

Self-Awareness is the first of four overall EQ domains.

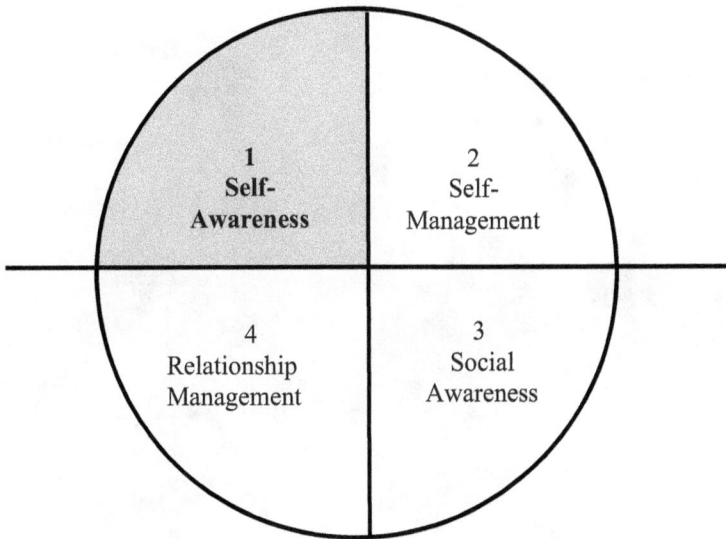

Self-Awareness embraces four aspects, which are covered in the chapters that follow:

- Recognising and naming feelings;
- Understanding emotions;
- Using an "Emotional Scale" to determine dominant emotions;
- Appraising yourself on the fourteen qualities of emotionally intelligent people.

Ray Laferla

2: RECOGNISING AND NAMING FEELINGS

Feelings are important because they reveal thoughts about how one thinks and what one values. Negative or uncomfortable feelings usually indicate that a need is not met or a value has been violated.

The word 'emotion' is derived from a Latin word that means 'to move'. Expressed feelings become emotions observed and seen by others in behaviours.

Feelings and emotions are, therefore, not random events. They are factors that reveal internal, causative elements at the root of human motivation.

Being aware of what we feel is essential for understanding ourselves and knowing what to do to act appropriately rather than improperly.

Let's take fear, for example. The emotion of fear could lead to three very different reactions:

- It may motivate a person to do something positive to alleviate the fear;
- It can paralyse or immobilise an individual to do nothing about it, hoping the problem will disappear;
- It could also cause someone to avoid what is feared.

These reactions happen spontaneously and automatically without rational thought and consideration.

An interesting observation is that unless people are conscious of the sentiment of fear and its consequences, they are inclined (by a factor of 10 to 1) to become either immobilised or avoid dealing with it. This means our emotions will likely trigger a disadvantageous and damaging unconscious response unless we are aware of what we are feeling and can control our behaviours.

On the other hand, if people are in touch with their feelings, they can look for the cause of their fear and consider ways of overcoming it. This is the emotionally intelligent response.

Being aware of feelings begins with the vocabulary and ability to name them. Without the capacity to label feelings, people can broadly say they are experiencing something without the ability to describe those feelings and comprehend their significance.

Five groups of feelings and emotions drive the vast majority of human behaviours. They are: mad, sad, glad, scared and other. Everything that does not fall under the first four categories is placed in the "other" category. The range of feelings in the five categories is listed in the table that follows:

Mad	Sad	Glad	Scared	Other
Angry	Blue	Amused	Afraid	Affectionate
Annoyed	Depressed	Comfortable	Agitated	Bored
Ashamed	Despondent	Content	Alone	Closed
Guilty	Discouraged	Ecstatic	Awkward	Co-operative
Irritated	Distressed	Lively	Concerned	Dumbfounded
Jealous	Down	Elated	Confused	Loving
Disappointed	Devastated	Excited	Distressed	Encouraged
Discouraged	Grief	Fascinated	Nervous	Bewildered
Frustrated	Hurt	Fulfilled	Forgetful	Forgiving
Furious	Lonely	Enthusiastic	Ignored	Fevered
Livid	Left out	Animated	Inhibited	Guileful

3: UNDERSTANDING EMOTIONS

Like feelings, emotions are indicators of what is occurring within ourselves. They are feedback mechanisms that tell us what we are experiencing internally and how we interpret situations.

By being aware of our emotions and labelling them, we can get in touch with how we perceive people and events. With this knowledge, we can understand what our feelings tell us to challenge irrational beliefs, change our thinking, get more information, or adapt to given situations.

For example, let's say that a woman fears heights. This adaptive fear helps her anticipate threats to her safety in order to take appropriate action. So when, for example, she stands back from the railing at the top of a tall building to appreciate the view, she does so to eliminate the risk of falling off the building due to the possibility of an unstable or insecure barrier.

Let's take another instance. Assume that a man has a volatile temperament and often expresses anger inappropriately. What are his emotions telling him? Perhaps he is a perfectionist and cannot tolerate mistakes or errors. It could be that he is rigid in his thinking and gets upset if anyone expresses a contrary view. Maybe he feels insecure and takes things personally whenever he receives negative feedback. He may also see himself as superior to others expecting them to defer to his opinions and treat him with deference. When they don't, he strikes out at them.

Many reasons could prompt the man to erupt in anger. If this person wishes to change or adapt his behaviours, the first thing to do is to ask why and when he gets angry. There will invariably be triggers that activate aggressive responses, which must be investigated to find adaptive solutions.

Emotionally intelligent people understand that emotions don't happen without some cognitive or thought process. By getting in touch with what we are thinking and linking that with how we feel, we can get to the root cause of many of our disturbances and take action to minimise or eradicate their occurrences. Let's consider the case of Amy as an example.

Amy's Story

Amy was a thirty-eight-year-old divorcee experiencing depression and a sense of hopelessness since her divorce two years before. She was lonely and struggling financially, with little joy or satisfaction.

One day, whilst travelling home from work during peak hour, she got extremely angry and frustrated in the traffic, which was moving at a snail's pace. For a moment, she reflected on her life and had an epiphany.

Amy knew she was unhappy and realised that no matter what happened to her, she remained with a feeling of despondency and despair nagging at her, dragging her down. She realised that she couldn't expect to feel different unless something changed. After all, Albert Einstein said that insanity is expecting a different outcome by doing the same thing repeatedly.

And so Amy got in touch with her feelings. They centred on the traffic at the time, and she felt angry and frustrated. She also recognised that her thoughts were negative and critical of everything, from how traffic moved to how people drove. She harboured thoughts such as:
- I hate this traffic jam:
- People drive like idiots;
- Nobody shows any courtesy on the roads anymore;
- The route shouldn't be so busy at this time;
- Who the hell does he think she is cutting in front of me (Amy thought this while she was hooting at the driver);

- I wouldn't need to drive my car if we had decent public transport.

With these thoughts, it's no wonder Amy felt angry and frustrated.

Then it occurred to Amy that she didn't have to be annoyed or frustrated. She could accept the motor gridlock without complaint, listen to music she liked, and plan a weekend that would appeal to her.

And so Amy relaxed while the traffic inched ahead. Soon she felt better. Later, at home, she turned her thoughts to other aspects of her life, such as the breakup of her marriage.

The last five years of their relationship were troubling and traumatic, with Amy's husband, Bill, having had several affairs. As things worsened, she knew they were headed for a divorce unless something changed. But nothing did.

Eventually, when Bill told Amy he was leaving her to live with another woman, she was deeply hurt. She experienced depression and despair that was still with her several years later.

Then Amy realised that the Friday afternoon traffic jam was a metaphor for her life. What did she feel about the breakup of her marriage, and how did she think about it? To Amy's discomfort, she realised that her feelings included rejection, betrayal, anger, resentment and guilt about letting her relationship deteriorate.

Amy's thoughts were primarily about criticising and condemning her ex-husband and bewailing her misfortunes.

Then Amy realised that she had to accept what she couldn't change (her divorce) and move on to a new future after learning from her failures and disappointments. Her emotions were telling her that the past was over. Instead of Amy identifying her former husband as the villain and herself as the victim, she could reframe her experience as both people coping the only way they knew how under the circumstances.

This insight lifted a load off Amy's shoulders. It was as though she had found a key that unlocked a chamber of her heart, where she had stored all the grudges, resentments and injustices of her married life. Now, she could open the door, let go of them, and be free.

Amy experienced a flood of tears and felt compassion for herself and forgiveness for the man she had married. She knew they were mismatched and couldn't live with one other, considering their differences in temperament, values and expectations. It would be better for both to be set free from this incompatible union, and it didn't matter who initiated it.

This insight motivated Amy to release the past and create a new future. Getting in touch with her emotions, understanding them, and taking action meant that her traumatic relationship served a beneficial purpose and that she need not preserve her festering wounds.

The day she was stuck in traffic, and in her life, Amy made a mental U-turn. She has since remarried and is happier than she has ever been. She has learned that her feelings are rooted in her thinking, and by reflecting on their meanings, she could take charge of her life and not be prey to circumstances.

Emotional Themes

Emotional themes are groups of emotions linked to one another. According to Paul Ekman, five primary emotional themes exist across all cultures, levels of education and income. They are:

- Pleasure;
- Sadness;
- Fear;
- Anger, and
- Disgust.

Pleasure

The emotion of pleasure comes from the expectation or experience of gain or satisfaction, which tells us that we are happy with events and circumstances.

Feelings of pleasure can be contrived if we focus on what is good and beneficial. One way of experiencing pleasure and satisfaction is to smile and embrace gratitude. In other words, consider the many things we can be grateful for instead of dwelling on wrongs, inequities and injustices.

Sadness

This emotion tells us that we are brooding on grievances, tribulations, disappointments, or the unfairness of situations.

The state of sadness ranges across many intensities of emotion, such as discouragement, resignation, hopelessness, despair, sorrow, anguish, grief and depression.

Fear

Fear is a psychological response to perceived danger. It triggers a survival response and often leads to the adaptive behaviours of fighting or escaping from the feared object, the well-known fight or flight response.

Aggression and avoidance are, therefore, two behaviours that may reveal conscious or unconscious fears.

Anger

We become angry when we believe that someone or something has interfered with our well-being and we are victims of injustice, insult or injury.

As with other emotions, the anger theme ranges across several emotional states, such as annoyance, frustration, argumentativeness, bitterness, hostility, fury and vengefulness. Anger moods include feeling irritable and impatient.

Disgust

Disgust is an evolutionary adaptation to keep us away from toxic behaviours or substances. Feeling sickened about something is an indicator telling us that an object or behaviour may be harmful. It is a response to something we find repulsive.

We may feel disgusted by many objects and behaviours, such as rotten food, stepping into excrement, seeing a child physically abused, looking at an infected, suppurating wound, etc.

We also feel disgusted when we hear about corrupt activities, sexual misdemeanours, flagrant sexism or racism, and other improprieties.

Conclusion

Emotions are messengers. They inform us how we are experiencing the world and whether we are dwelling on the positive or negative aspects of events and circumstances.

When frequently experiencing adverse emotions, it would behove us to examine our thoughts. Perhaps we need to reframe circumstances, let go of the past, forgive ourselves and others, accept what we cannot change, moderate our expectations, or practice tolerance. We must also recognise that people are flawed and understand that we live in an imperfect world where we will often be frustrated and disappointed.

By tuning into our emotions and understanding their messages, we can act appropriately to free ourselves from their afflictions.

4: EMOTIONAL LEVELS AND IDENTIFYING DOMINANT EMOTIONS

Using the Emotional Scale to Identify Dominant Emotions

The Emotional Scale is a guidance system developed by Dr David Hawkins. Its purpose is to provide a method for evaluating where we are in a range from the lowest level (e.g. shame) to the highest point (e.g. joy).

The table that follows is an adaption of the original Emotional Scale, slightly modified to accommodate the tenets of EQ. It groups emotions into ten categories or levels, ranging from the most powerful and beneficial (3) to the most dysfunctional and disempowering (-6).

Level	Emotional State
3	Joy, Love, Appreciation, Serenity
2	Enthusiasm, Gratitude
1	Optimism, Helpfulness
0	Rationality
-1	Boredom
-2	Arrogance, Frustration, Disappointment
-3	Discouragement, Pessimism, Anxiety
-4	Anger, Hostility, Animosity, Bitterness
-5	Jealousy, Envy, Insecurity, Guilt, Fear
-6	Shame, Depression, Hopefulness, Grief, Despair, Unworthiness

Referring to the table, notice that the further down we go from 0 (Rationality is the turning point), the greater the negativity and disablement of emotion. From zero up, all emotions are positive.

By familiarising ourselves with the Emotional Scale and being aware of where we are on this scale, we can choose to move from a current level towards a more enabling state. Unfortunately, if we are unaware of the state of our dominant emotions, we are unlikely to do anything about changing them. Therefore, the starting point for change is knowing where we are on the Emotional Scale at any given time. With this in mind, we are able to move up the scale to more empowering levels.

Raising Emotional Levels

Earlier, you were introduced to the ten emotional levels, from the most debilitating states (shame etc.) to the most empowering states (joy, love, etc.). The question now is, how do you elevate yourself from a lower negative state to a better one?

There are four steps to climbing the emotional ladder:

- Become aware of your dominant emotional state;
- Take responsibility for changing it;
- Formulate a strategy for moving up the emotional scale;
- Take action.

1. Become Aware Of Your Emotional State

Let's assume that something has happened that makes you feel bad. You are experiencing distress and don't feel like doing anything. You want to withdraw and retreat into yourself without concern for anybody or anything. You have little energy and feel like sleeping and disengaging from life.

If you had to use a name to describe your feeling, you might call it 'depression'. Specifying your emotional state lets you see that depression is at the lowest level (-6) on the Emotional Scale.

2. Take Responsibility

You are ultimately responsible for the quality of your life. This is a principle you must embrace to be happy and experience fulfilment. There is always the temptation to blame others for your feelings and misfortunes, but that perspective serves no positive purpose. If anything, it worsens the situation.

Taking responsibility for your actions, choices and direction in life is the most practical and intelligent way of dealing with issues. When you abdicate responsibility, you are powerless because the solution to a problem appears outside your influence or control.

When you take responsibility, you become respons-able. Your ability to respond enables you to either do something about the issue, or accept the situation and move on.

Remember that you are a human being who can choose your emotions and behaviours. You are not a puppet. Decide to think and act wisely. Refuse to stay in a highly charged negative state of mind.

3. Formulate A Strategy For Moving Up The Emotional Scale

Many words describe feelings and emotions, but you can boil it down to two core feelings: one feels good, the other bad.

The highest state of mind feels good and experiences joy, love, appreciation, serenity, enthusiasm, gratitude, optimism, and hopefulness.

But how can you get to these states?

First, if you are at the three lowest levels (-6 to -4) on the Emotional Scale, do not try to elevate your state to the top three levels (optimism, enthusiasm, joy); the gap is too big to bridge in one leap. A better strategy is to move from a negative state to the mindset of being rational, which is the level of neutrality (0).

One way to do this is to apply rational thinking to manage emotions. This is addressed in Chapter 11.

Another strategy you can use is to establish your emotion's algorithm or formula and use it to bring about the required change. The equation in the algorithm provides the antecedent, or precursor, of the outcome. So, if $2 + 2 = 4$, four is the result of the antecedent, $2 + 2$. So too, with emotions.

The following list consists of algorithms applicable to seven major emotions:

- ➤ Anxiety = Uncertainty x Powerlessness;
- ➤ Disappointment = Expectations – Reality;
- ➤ Endogenous Depression = Suffering – Meaning;
- ➤ Discouragement = Disappointment + Apathy;
- ➤ Fear = Apprehension x Perceived Danger;
- ➤ Regrets = Disappointment + Self-blame;
- ➤ Shame = Humiliation + Self-condemnation.

Now that you have some emotional equations to work with, how do you use them to overcome adverse conditions? Let's take depression as an example.

If you know that the formula for depression is suffering without meaning, you can reframe the situation and find significance in an otherwise disturbing event (or series of events). Simply asking, "What can I learn from this?" to find something beneficial in a situation makes it meaningful. At this point, suffering diminishes. We may be left with sadness (the event may still be upsetting), but that's a far cry from being depressed.

While talking about depression, bear in mind that there are essentially two types:

- Endogenous; and
- Reactive.

Endogenous depression occurs from a chemical or hormonal imbalance in the body. For example, post-partum depression occurs in women after delivering a baby; it is a hormonal condition for women adjusting to childbirth. Many clinical depressions are also triggered by hormonal or chemical imbalances that require medical interventions.

On the other hand, if the depression is reactive, it occurs in response to a specific event. This psychological condition may be addressed by using the method described in Chapter 11.

Another technique to alter your mental state is to change your physiology. Decide on the tone and pace of your voice, and other physical characteristics congruent with how you want to feel, and display those, even if you fake it at first. More details about this aspect are provided in Chapter 7.

4. Take Action

Having a plan, important as it is, is not enough. A strategy must be executed and action taken. This is the essential requirement of any successful endeavour. You no longer worry and obsess about the issue when you take action. You look past the problem and do something about what you want to achieve. This is liberating.

Also, taking action is empowering. A disempowering situation exists when people do nothing and have no options. As long as there are alternatives, there are opportunities. And with opportunities comes hope.

Ray Laferla

28

5: FIFTEEN QUALITIES OF EMOTIONALLY INTELLIGENT PEOPLE

Emotional Intelligence is the ability to navigate the volatile world of emotions and direct your feelings to achieve desired results.

Essentially EQ means being aware of your feelings and how behaviours affect people, both positively and negatively. It also involves managing and controlling emotions, especially when stressed or under pressure.

People with high Emotional Intelligence need to display all fifteen attributes that follow. Study these attributes to check how you rate in each of them. Any shortcoming is a characteristic you need to work on to raise your EQ.

1. Practise Self-Awareness

The opposite of self-awareness is being oblivious to your feelings, and reacting impulsively and spontaneously to adverse situations and troublesome people. Such people are often perceived as volatile and inconsistent, sometimes called 'firecrackers' because a small disruption can set them off.

2. Practice Empathy

Empathy is the ability to sense and understand what people are feeling. To do so, we must have the capacity to see things from the perspective of others.

There are two types of empathy:

    i.   *Affective empathy* refers to the sensations and feelings we experience when we are in rapport with people. In other words, we feel what other people are feeling;

ii.   ***Cognitive empathy*** takes place when we understand the emotions of others, even though we do not experience them ourselves.

Emotionally intelligent people can interpret the signals that others present. These people observe sensory and emotional cues that enable them to look beyond what a person says to how an individual feels.

Empathy is an important quality to possess. It facilitates understanding and compassion and enables people to provide support in appropriate ways. It also plays an important role in motivating others to give their best.

The subject of empathy is covered more fully in Chapter 13.

3. Be Trustworthy

Trust is integral to any relationship, whether with customers, colleagues, subordinates, friends, or family. No one is willing to reveal any ideas, thoughts, aspirations, and feelings that make themselves vulnerable, unless trust exists between the parties.

Emotionally intelligent people are careful to act authentically and consistently, knowing it takes a long time to build trust and a few seconds to destroy it.

The following behaviours will prevent the building of trust and should be avoided:

×   Self-serving practices that take advantage of others;
×   Lies and deceit;
×   Prejudice or bias;
×   Inconsistency;
×   Arrogance;
×   Lack of courage to say and do the right thing;
×   Betrayal of confidences;
×   Intentional wrongdoing;
×   Making promises and not keeping them.

On the other hand, to be trusted, a manager must always be:
- ✓ Considerate of others,
- ✓ Fair and unbiased,
- ✓ Courageous (brave enough to do what is right, not convenient),
- ✓ Consistent,
- ✓ Genuine and sincere,
- ✓ Supportive,
- ✓ Ethical, with a clear moral code, and
- ✓ Dependable.

4. Refuse To Harbour Resentment

Resentment is holding on to feelings of bitterness or animosity against someone who has treated you poorly or harmed you. These feelings usually remain long after incidents occur and are a common source of human suffering.

Because people justify holding on to resentment, there is an emotional attachment to the feeling. It can, therefore, be challenging to want to release it by forgiving the perpetrator.

A highly effective process for practising forgiveness is provided in Chapter 12.

5. Don't Take Criticism Personally

We all have weaknesses, some of which irritate and annoy others, resulting in disparaging comments. Furthermore, when we fail to respond the way others expect us to, people are disposed to criticise our behaviours. Even our strengths can be a source of complaint because some people may begrudge our gifts and talents.

Dale Carnegie said in his book, How to Win Friends and Influence People: *"Unjust criticism is usually a disguised compliment. It often means you have aroused jealously and envy. Remember that no one ever kicks a dead dog"*.

Emotionally intelligent people know they should never take criticism personally, so they remain rational and do not overreact.

Whenever people criticise you, consider the source. Does that individual know you well? Do you respect the views of that person? Was the comment made to hurt you during a heated argument? Does the critical person often behave irrationally, verbally attacking anybody who upsets him/her?

Also, consider the validity of the criticism. Can you learn something from the comment made? If the complaint is invalid, disregard the criticism, bearing in mind the prejudice of the antagonist. On the other hand, if critical remarks are valid, be thankful for them, even if it hurts. Resolve to correct the matter, and you will be a better person for it.

6. Be An Independent Thinker (Don't Follow The Crowd)

Each of us is an individual, unique and distinct, with different talents and skills.

While we all want to express our exclusivity, we also seek the approval and acceptance of others. And so, we are disposed to accept the opinions and endorsements of groups of people, doing what they do and thinking how they think. However, by following the crowd, we deny our individuality and are likely to end up where most people end up, in a place called average or mediocrity.

We need to be aware of how group behaviour affects us if we are to think independently and express our distinctiveness. Most people are insecure and unhappy, and they reflect this by adopting common behaviours so that nobody confronts them with their shortcomings.

A crowd of people is less able to arrive at rational judgments than individuals who think independently and seek facts. This is because dominant group members usually exert the most influence over the majority, which follows mindlessly.

It takes courage to think individually and differ from others in a group, even when your ideas are valid and constructive. If you are the only dissenter, you may be overruled and disregarded as a team player.

An example is the disaster that occurred on 29 January 1986, when the space shuttle Challenger exploded seventy-three seconds into its flight, killing all seven astronauts.

The tragedy was caused by the failure of two O-ring seals joining one of the rocket boosters. The low temperatures at the time of the launch reduced the elasticity of the rubber O-rings, impacting their ability to seal joints.

A Presidential Commission was established to investigate the cause of the accident. They found that NASA's managers wanted to go ahead with a launch that the engineers of Morton Thiokol, the manufacturer of the rocket boosters, did not agree with. With few exceptions, the engineers buckled under NASA's pressure and eventually consented to a launch against their better judgment. The exception was Roger Boisjoly, one of the designers of the rocket boosters, who was vindicated when the shuttle exploded.

It isn't easy to think independently and not submit to the vested interests of a select group who are influential. Yet this is one of the attributes of a courageous person with a high EQ.

7. Live A Balanced Life

Emotionally intelligent people know that what we neglect deteriorates. It's easy to observe this with physical possessions and material things. That's why we regularly service our motor vehicles, maintain our homes, etc.

However, what is often overlooked is that, unless maintained or improved, even non-physical things, including skills and relationships, change for the worse.

The second law of thermodynamics, the Law of Entropy, says that everything continually deteriorates, and preventing obsolescence or disintegration requires maintenance and renewal. From bodies to buildings, things will worsen unless preserved.

Consequently, maintaining a healthy work/life balance is critically important for our well-being. What value are wealth, status, and power if we lose the love and support of our family, if our health deteriorates, and if we do not enjoy our achievements because we are always clamouring for more, and neglect the things that money cannot buy? Spending much time in one area of our lives and neglecting other important aspects will lead to regret.

So, devote sufficient time to your spouse, children, relatives, and friends. Also, remember that a balanced lifestyle includes getting adequate sleep, maintaining a healthy diet, relaxing, and exercising.

8. Don't Fixate On The Past

People with a high EQ learn from the past but don't dwell on it. They have no time for regrets, shame, guilt, or remorse. It does not mean these people don't take responsibility for past behaviours. Rather, it means they are conscious that the past is over and cannot be undone.

The only value past mistakes have is what we can learn from them, which can make us better people by enabling us not to repeat blunders. So, gain insights and knowledge from mistakes and move on to create an exciting future.

9. Manage Emotions And Express Them Appropriately

At the core of EQ is the ability to control and direct emotions appropriately. We must be aware of our feelings and remain rational and calm in the face of adverse events and unpleasant people.

This does not mean we are docile and passive, bemoaning fate and letting people say and do what they like, no matter how repugnant. Instead, EQ enables us to consider the cause of abhorrent or irrational behaviour and focus on finding solutions in a composed state of mind.

In Chapter 11, we will explore how people can apply rational thinking and reach sound conclusions to direct and channel emotions in productive ways. Where events cannot be controlled or influenced, the solution is to accept the situation without resentment and move on.

10. Be Adaptable

Emotionally intelligent people know when to persist with a course of action and when to quit and do something different. Although persistence is a noteworthy trait, it is also foolish to continue hitting your head against a brick wall when change is needed. But how can you know when to stick with something or surrender and move on?

When your plans are not working, first adapt and refine them. If these actions fail, and you reach the stage where you have exhausted all reasonable possibilities, you must admit that you have arrived at a dead end. At this stage, inflexibility and stubbornness can lead to ruin.

Throughout life, we choose which path to take from various routes available to us. Sometimes we take the right road and end where we want to go. At other times we take the wrong road that leads nowhere or to a bad place. It's prudent, therefore, to realise that it is never too late to change direction or turn around. We can start again and learn from our mistakes.

Being adaptable, without giving up easily, is a valuable attribute to have. Stay open-minded and be willing to adapt when necessary. Remember that whatever you do, keep going, even if it means changing direction. Never stop in your quest to achieve goals. If you do, you will likely succumb to discouragement, despondency and idleness.

11. Remain Calm Under Pressure

Most people encounter life and work pressures to a lesser or greater degree. There is seldom enough time, people, or resources to enable people to live in an unhurried and relaxed manner. Consequently, we are frequently on edge, battling to cope with deadlines and the many demands placed upon us.

In a recent study, 94% of people reported high stress levels at work. This problem is not, however, confined to office hours. About 54% of respondents said they take work home several times a week, limiting their time with children and spouses. This practice causes stress and resentment because it forces the neglect of familial relationships.

When stressed, our brains and bodies stop working in an organised and calm manner because we are in a state of agitation, restlessness, and exasperation. This affects the quality and accuracy of our work, resulting in mistakes. We also become agitated when people interrupt us or fail to respond quickly to our requests.

There are three simple actions we can take to cope with everyday pressures:

i. *Pause and breathe deeply*

Deep breathing, also known as diaphragmatic breathing, is a well-known way of centering yourself to release anxiety when feeling uptight. It is a technique often used by public speakers, singers and actors who feel nervous before going on stage.

Deep breathing is breathing from the diaphragm at the bottom of the lungs. If you place your hand on your stomach while you breathe in, your hand should move out with the expansion of your lungs. Conversely, when you breathe out, you should see your hand go in with each exhale.

Breathe deeply in and out about seven times, pausing at the top of each breath for a few seconds.

ii. *Break tasks down into small chunks*

A large project contains a series of manageable actions which, if carried out sequentially, will ensure its achievement.

Desmond Tutu once remarked, *"There is only one way to eat an elephant: a bite at a time"*. Tutu meant that everything that appears daunting or overwhelming is accomplished by undertaking several small tasks, one after the other. This is the antidote to feeling crushed by the weight of a large assignment.

iii. *Allocate uninterrupted time to focus on important matters.*

When work pressure is severe, with deadlines to meet, allocating a specific amount of uninterrupted time for working on important issues is helpful. You must make yourself unavailable during this period unless a crisis demands your immediate attention.

During your reserved time, do not receive phone calls. Instead, take messages which you will respond to later. Remember that the purpose of uninterrupted time is to focus your attention on getting as much work done as possible without being hampered by disruptions.

12. Live One Day At A Time

Thomas Carlyle, a 19th century philosopher, once said, *"Our main business is not to see what lies dimly at a distance but to do what lies clearly at hand"*. These words profoundly affected the life of Sir William Osler, the man regarded as the father of modern medicine.

In an address to students at Yale University, Osler said that his achievements lay not in *"brains of a special quality"* but in what he called *"living in day-tight compartments"*. This phrase refers to the technique used in shipbuilding to seal off various parts of a ship from one another. So, if a ship's hull is pierced or ripped apart, allowing the sea to rush in, large water-tight doors come down to isolate segments of the vessel. This action keeps the water confined to prevent the ship from sinking.

Sir William Osler said: *"Each of you is much more marvellous than a great liner, and you are bound on a longer voyage. I urge you to learn to live in 'day-tight compartments' as a most certain way to ensure safety on your voyage [through life]. Touch a button and hear, at every level of your life, iron doors shutting out the past – the dead yesterdays. Touch another and shut off the future – the unborn tomorrows. Then you are safe, safe for today"*.

When you stop and think about it, a lifetime is a succession of days, one after another, strung into weeks, months, and years. Take care of each day, and you take care of your life. Succeed one day at a time, and a successful life will follow naturally.

Sir Osler's words are wise; live in the present and take one day at a time. Make the most of your time by focusing only on today's work and doing it as best you can. You don't have to neglect thinking about the future. Plan for tomorrow by all means, but live in the present, one day at a time.

13. Maintain An Attitude Of Gratitude
We live at a time of unprecedented advances in all walks of life, from incredible technologies to an amazing array of mind-blowing goods and huge medical advancements. Yet most of us take these for granted.

If we consider our lives from the viewpoint of our ancestors, we can conclude that we have never been more comfortable. Never have we been more educated, with more choices available to us. We have constant information, communication streams and entertainment at our disposal and live lives of relative ease. Yet more people are depressed, as revealed by the volumes of tranquillisers and anti-depressants prescribed by physicians. Why is this so?

The reasons are that our expectations have increased, and we have an attitude of entitlement. When we get into a car and drive on a smooth asphalt road, we don't think of how it used to be riding a horse or carriage. The discomfort and slow pace of this bygone means of transport does not enter our awareness. Instead, we compare our vehicles to bigger and better models and are annoyed when confronted with the slightest inconvenience.

In the same way, we take for granted the many blessings we experience and are unaware of the freedoms, opportunities, and amenities we enjoy.

The consequence of this frame of reference is that we focus on having more of what we desire and not appreciating or enjoying what we possess.

By maintaining an attitude of gratitude, we reconnect with the advantages and benefits we experience. We appreciate the good fortune in our lives, not only in terms of physical possessions but also in mental and relationship fortuity.

Professor Robert A. Emmons, editor-in-chief of the Journal of Positive Psychology, says that gratitude can transform people's lives for many reasons. For example:

- It helps people focus on the present;
- It plays a role in acquiring positive emotions;
- It improves self-worth;
- People feel happier;
- Life becomes more meaningful;
- People enjoy the things they have;
- It puts life into perspective;
- It contributes to decreased stress;
- It promotes better immunity and health;
- It helps people get through hard times;
- People are less susceptible to anxiety and depression;
- It leads to more fulfilling relationships.

14. Maintain A Sense Of Gratitude

There are several things you can do to experience a sense of gratitude:

- Spend a few moments each day thinking about the things you can be thankful for;
- Pause to marvel at the wonder of nature, such as a sunset, a beautiful natural scene, an exquisite flower, a magnificent garden, etc.;
- Be thankful for your mental and physical health. If you are receiving treatment for a disease or illness, appreciate the medication and healthcare services available to help you;

- Marvel at the wonder of modern life, such as television, air travel, the internet, smartphones, computers, and entertainment platforms;
- Be appreciative of the priceless value of loving relationships, including your spouse, children, extended family and friends;
- List at least ten specific things you can be thankful for, and keep this in your wallet or handbag. Refer to this list at least once a day before you retire for the night. Create a new list each month;
- Reframe experiences. See adversity as something you can benefit or learn from. If we look back at our lives, most of us, with hindsight, can see that even our most traumatic experiences profit us in the long run. Olivia Newton-John, who struggled with cancer for over thirty years and eventually succumbed to it, said: *"Cancer got me over unimportant fears, like getting old. I look at my cancer journey as a gift. It made me slow down and realise the important things in life and taught me not to sweat the small stuff"*;
- Keep a "gratitude stone" with you. Several times a day, touch the stone and think of a least one thing for which you can be grateful. At the end of the day, place the stone on your bedside table and consider all the good things you experienced that day.

15. Embrace Change

Change is an inevitable part of life. Emotionally intelligent managers are aware of this, knowing that things are constantly evolving or regressing.

Embracing change necessitates increasing our knowledge and skills, being open to new experiences, embracing new technologies, adapting to changes in society, and remaining relevant in a fast-changing world.

RAISING EMOTIONAL INTELLIGENCE

The Second Domain of EQ: Self-Management

Ray Laferla

RAISING EMOTIONAL INTELLIGENCE
Self-Management

Self-Management is the second of the four overall EQ competencies.

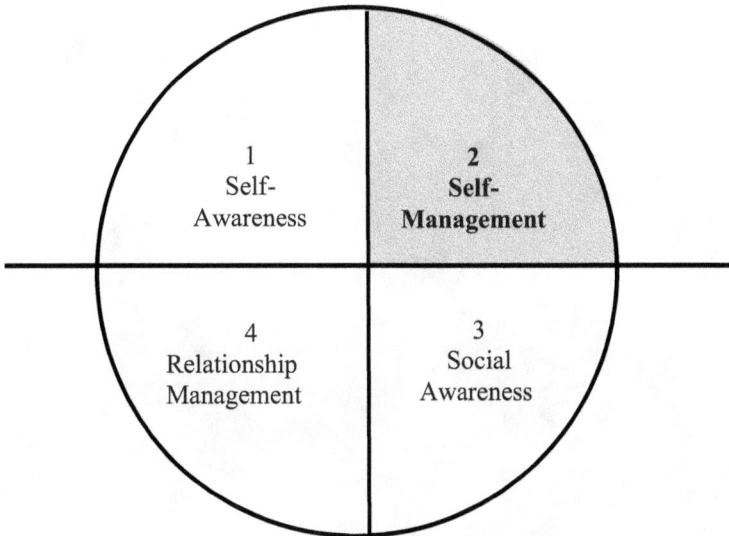

In the chapters that follow, we will provide you with the know-how to acquire seven skills to manage yourself and your emotions. They are:
- Implementing a strategy for successful achievement;
- Using physiology to create an empowering mental state;
- Applying self-discipline;
- Building resilience and mental toughness;
- Forming good habits and overcoming bad ones;
- Applying rational thinking to manage emotions;
- Engaging forgiveness to achieve emotional freedom.

Ray Laferla

6: IMPLEMENTING A STRATEGY FOR SUCCESSFUL ACHIEVEMENT

Success, in any form, seldom occurs by luck or accident. To achieve anything worthwhile, we must commit ourselves to do whatever is needed, for however long it may take. In other words, success requires sacrifice, and we must dedicate ourselves to a specific goal. This sounds easy, but why do most people live ordinary lives without much significance if it is so simple?

The reason is that people want to be successful but don't know how; they don't have a strategy. Furthermore, even with a plan, they do not apply essential, overarching values to attain their goals. In other words, the paradigm for achieving success comprises two parts:

- The application of *overarching values*; and
- Implementing a *strategy for success*.

1. Overarching Values

Several values are of great benefit to humanity: virtues such as honesty, love, boldness, fairness, optimism, loyalty and many others. As beneficial as these may be, only two overarching values are at the core of all meaningful achievement. They are self-control and perseverance.

Self-control

Remember that we only succeed through consistent and focused effort, usually over months or years, requiring self-control and discipline.

Albert Gray once gave a highly acclaimed presentation called *"The Common Denominator of Success"*. After researching the subject for many years, Gray concluded that success is not due to wealth, intelligence, education, opportunity, or any such factor. The only common denominator he found was that successful people consistently applied self-control to achieve their goals. He said that achievers developed the *"habit of doing the things that others did not like to do"*.

And what do people not like to do? They don't like applying themselves to unpleasant tasks, preferring to engage in diversionary activities. So, the successful student who enjoys partying with friends chooses to study instead. The manager who doesn't feel like completing her report gets on with it and refuses to procrastinate. A would-be athlete, who finds training a chore, resolves to train, even though he dislikes it, etc.

Doing what you don't like to do, to achieve what you desire, means disciplining yourself to take action when you don't feel like it; no significant success is possible without such self-control.

Perseverance

Success is never a straight line moving upwards. It is a winding road with many ups and downs, roadblocks and setbacks. To keep going, we need to persevere.

Perseverance is not giving up when the going gets tough. It is steadfastly enduring the delays, impediments and obstacles on your chosen path.

J.K. Rowling, author of the Harry Potter series of books, sent her manuscript to twelve publishers who refused her work. But rejection didn't deter her, and she continued to seek a book producer in the face of apparent failure. Eventually, Bloomsbury decided to publish Rowling's work, and the rest is history. Together, the series of Harry Potter books have sold about 500 million copies, making it the best-selling book of all time after The Bible.

Failure to find a publisher did not deter Rowling. She steadfastly persisted and refused to give up. When asked what she did to keep going in the face of apparent defeat, she said: *"I stopped pretending that I was anything other than what I was, and began to direct all my energy into finishing the only work that mattered to me".* By persisting with her writing, and finding a publisher to distribute the book, Rowling became the most successful author of all time.

Be aware that nobody achieves success overnight. The road to achievement is a difficult journey with many obstacles to overcome. Most people are excited to begin moving towards their goals but become discouraged when things get tough.

On the other hand, high achievers expect to encounter problems, and when they do, they apply their minds to overcoming challenges and continuing to move forward with grit and perseverance.

2. Implementing A Strategy For Success

Successful achievement is the outcome of implementing a four-step strategy. This concept is illustrated in the diagram below:

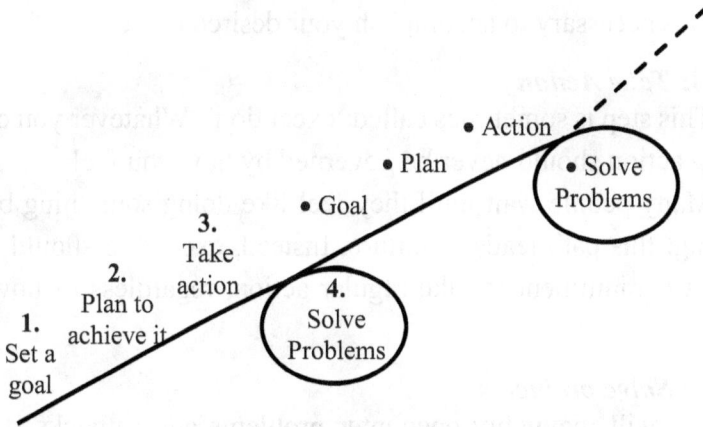

Step 1: Set a goal. Know precisely what you want to achieve

Your goal must be specific and measurable.

Unlike objectives related to business, I recommend that you do not set a time limit for personal goals.

At work, we spend at least eight hours each day, devoting whatever time we need to achieve business goals with company resources at our disposal. At home, however, we have much less time to give to many matters such as family, recreation, home maintenance, social activities, sports, etc., all of which require our attention.

Notwithstanding not setting time limits, you must still give your personal goal the attention it deserves. To do this, allocate some time each weekday, no matter how small, to achieve your goal. The cumulative effect of this action will surprise you, and you will enjoy a more balanced, productive, and happier lifestyle by not focusing obsessively on one thing to the detriment of your family and other needs.

Step 2: Formulate an Action Plan

An Action Plan is a sequence of actions to achieve an objective.

To formulate a plan, specify your objective. Then list all the things you need to do to achieve your goal. If you are unsure of what actions to take, be prepared to consult with others familiar with the methods necessary to accomplish your desired outcome.

Step 3: Take Action

This step is sometimes called 'execution'. Whatever you call it, taking action should never be governed by how you feel.

Many people wait until they feel like doing something before moving; this path leads to failure. Instead, execution should come from a commitment to take regular action, regardless of how one feels.

Step 4: Solve problems

You will inevitably encounter problems and setbacks if your goal is ambitious enough. These obstacles can have serious consequences and may prevent you from reaching your goal. It is, therefore, essential that you overcome any problems you may encounter.

To solve problems, follow this proven six-step procedure:
- Establish the apparent problem;
- Get facts and ask questions (why, where, when, what, who

and how) to identify the real problem;
- Consider possible solutions (options);
- Weigh up the pros and cons of each option;
- Make the decision;
- Follow-through.

When you have solved your immediate problem, it is important to recycle the success strategy (goal, plan, action and problem-solving) and keep going until you accomplish your objective.

7: USING PHYSIOLOGY TO CREATE EMPOWERING MENTAL STATES

Your body is a powerful medium for expressing feelings you constantly communicate through facial expressions, posture, voice, and general demeanour.

Knowing that there is a physical expression for every feeling you experience is important. Emotions such as anger, depression, fear, and happiness can be seen in your physiology, even when you endeavour to hide your feelings from others.

Because posture and feelings align themselves with one another, physiology is a powerful tool for changing mental states. When you are run down, your positive energy is low. Conversely, your mental state is enthusiastic and vibrant when your body is highly charged and energetic.

You cannot experience emotion without a corresponding alignment of physiology. So, one way to change your state of mind is to change your physiology. If, therefore, you smile and act cheerfully, you will soon start to feel better, even though you may have started out feeling miserable. Good actors and movie stars experience this change in mental state every time they take on a character.

When Charlize Theron assumed the role of Aileen Wournos in the movie 'Monster', she had to think and act like a prostitute and serial killer who had murdered six men. She also had to look like Wournos. So, she shaved her eyebrows, packed on thirty pounds, donned prosthetic teeth and behaved like a crude, abused, angry and bitter person.

It wasn't long before Charlize began to feel like Wournos.

Throughout the making of the movie, she felt like the woman she was pretending to be.

Charlize portrayed the character of Aileen so convincingly that critics said she played it to perfection. Except that Charlize didn't play Wournos, she was Wournos. She felt the feelings and experienced the traumatic emotions of a maltreated, betrayed, and bad-tempered killer. Theron did this by taking on the physiology of the murderer, expressing them so convincingly that she won both a Golden Globe Award and an Oscar for her acting.

Just as an actor can become the person whose role she is assuming, you and I can become the person we want to be by taking on the requisite physiology.

If you want to be happier, put a smile on your face, walk with a spring in your step, talk enthusiastically, and soon you will feel good. If you want to feel confident, breathe deeply and act confidently.

The aphorism, "fake it until you make it", is true from a biological point of view. Perhaps William James (the father of modern psychology) said it best: *"Our actions guide our emotions. If you want a characteristic, act as if you already have it"*. He also said, *"Feelings trigger actions just as actions trigger feelings"*.

When using your physiology to control or redirect your feelings, remember that there are five expressions of body language:

- Facial appearance (e.g. a smile, interest, enthusiasm, etc.);
- Tone of voice;
- Eye contact;
- Posture;
- Use of hands.

Let's now examine each in more detail.

Facial Appearance

Facial appearance is probably the most basic aspect of our physiology because our expressions reveal our feelings.

Smiling makes us feel good; it creates a body sensation of approval, pleasure, and well-being. While experiencing these emotions, we also communicate them to others, resulting in a return of positive feelings.

Tone of Voice

Your tonality will create inner sensations ranging from calmness to agitation and anger. Talk loudly and aggressively, and your tone will make you feel belligerent. Alternatively, speaking calmly and firmly will make you feel confident and resolute in communicating your message.

If you speak falsely, like an American trying to emulate a British aristocrat with airs and graces, you'll feel uncomfortable because those expressions will not come naturally to you. So, always use a tone of voice that is natural, warm and caring.

Eye Contact

Your eyes reveal a great deal of what is taking place within you. For example, by looking down, you show that you are experiencing embarrassment or shame.

People who avoid eye contact usually feel a lack of confidence and express themselves accordingly. So, by making good eye contact, you will feel more confident and engaged.

This advice is also relevant when communicating over electronic media, such as Zoom or Microsoft Teams. Look at the camera, wherever it is located, and not at the image in the corner of the screen. This will convey the impression that you are looking directly at the recipient, and not down to your side. Remember that looking into the eyes of people does not mean staring. You don't want to overdo it. Just be natural.

Posture

The posture you adopt reflects your mental state. For example, when you feel sad or unhappy, your shoulders slump. To feel better, change your physiology to reflect a more resourceful condition. You can do this by standing tall, throwing your shoulders back, looking forward and upward and breathing deeply. Move energetically and let your posture emphatically express confidence and assurance. This will transform your mental state from sadness to optimism.

You can also use a "power pose" by placing your hands on your hips or leaning forward over a table (or desk) with spread-out hands on the tabletop.

Hands

Like every other part of our body, our hands align with how we feel and can be used to make us feel better and impact others. Here are some suggestions on how to use our hands.

The handshake

In the Western world, when we introduce ourselves by shaking hands.

In a neutral handshake, both parties exert equal pressure. In an unequal relationship, the person who seeks to demonstrate superiority will usually exert greater strength by forcefully gripping the other person's hand. This person will also likely turn the other person's hand down, i.e., underneath.

The way, therefore, to feel equal and establish equivalence with a handshake is to adhere to two rules: keep your hand vertical (straight up) and apply the same pressure you receive.

Using your hands during a presentation

Hands are important to any presenter or person making a speech, and they unconsciously convey information that may enhance or detract from a presentation. By consciously using your hands in a specific manner, you feel positive and comfortable with your audience and will communicate these emotions to them.

With this in mind, here are some guidelines:
- Palms in an upward position convey an impression of openness, genuineness and friendliness;

- Palms down is a power signal. It suggests dominance and the expectation that others will accept what is being said and obey commands. Most people unconsciously resist speakers who gesticulate with their palms facing the floor.
- A third way in which hands may be used is to point fingers. This is an aggressive posture and is likely to evoke an audience's negative reaction, or at least a feeling of discomfort;
- Another way to use your hands when making a presentation or conversing with others is to place the open fingers of one hand against the open fingers of the other hand. In other words, it looks like a prayerful position, except that the touching fingers are spread apart. This position makes the speaker look confident and in charge, but not arrogant.

When being introduced to others, adopt a considerate and decisive mental attitude, and let your handshake express it. Your handshake should be firm (neither soft nor hard) to reflect a balanced and friendly disposition.

8: APPLYING SELF-DISCIPLINE

Many qualities can improve a person's life, such as being a likeable character, honesty, trustworthiness etc. However, there is one attribute that, more than any other single factor, will ensure sustainable, long-term success. That attribute is self-discipline.

Whether you desire to achieve goals, maintain good relationships, enjoy a healthy lifestyle or succeed in life, self-discipline is the trait most needed to accomplish anything worthwhile.

According to a 2013 study by Wilhelm Hoffman from the University of Chicago, disciplined people are happier and more successful than those lacking restraint. This is because self-disciplined people are better able to deal with temptations. They don't give in to their feelings and spend little time considering whether to indulge in pleasing rather than productive behaviours. In other words, those who exercise self-discipline do not allow impulses or emotions to dictate their choices. Instead, they make decisions that drive their actions to achieve goals.

Self-discipline is a learned behaviour, and we must internalise it as a habit. After you ingrain this habit, you will automatically do what needs to be done without experiencing the inner conflict of deciding between a pleasurable or less enjoyable activity. You will, without thinking, move yourself to action regardless of how you feel.

Perhaps the best way to acquire self-discipline is to apply three principles to everyday situations: finish whatever you begin, do your best in everything you undertake, and go the extra mile. These require effort and are excellent ways of internalising positive habits that will serve you well.

1. Finish Whatever You Start

It's very easy to start projects but much more difficult to see them through to the end, especially when you have lost the desire to continue or when things get boring or difficult.

Adopting the principle of finishing what you start makes you mindful of what you take on because you will be stuck with it until completion. This means that every book you read, every assignment you accept, and everything you begin will require a commitment to action until completion.

This principle also applies to recurring or continuing events such as maintaining your house, mentoring someone, coaching a school team, weeding your garden, etc. Every time you commit to a task, accept the obligation of staying with it to its conclusion.

2. Do Your Best In Everything You Undertake

Applying your best efforts means you don't take shortcuts that may compromise the quality of your work.

Always doing your best takes effort, especially when you feel demotivated, tired, or pressured to complete something quickly. Under these circumstances, it takes self-discipline not to compromise your standards.

The habit of always doing your best will have four beneficial consequences:

- You feel good about yourself and your work, knowing you did not give in to expediency. Your self-esteem is thus enhanced;
- People know you are committed to excellence, which boosts your reputation;
- You are trusted. When new, exciting and unusual projects are assigned, you will likely be offered them first, confirming the faith leaders have in you;
- Your best will improve as you develop greater skills and

become more competent. This will make you more valuable to your company and enhance your career prospects.

3. Go The Extra Mile

Going the extra mile is the act of doing more than expected. It necessitates making a special effort to give more than required, creating additional value for others.

Providing additional value is the difference between average employees and top performers. Achievers go beyond the call of duty to do more than the minimum. And they go the extra mile for three reasons:

- By going beyond the call of duty, staff find meaning and satisfaction because they perform their activities to provide the greatest possible benefit to those they serve. Consequently, they feel good about themselves, especially when they get positive feedback;
- The work people do expresses who they are and reflects their values. People who value themselves are not content producing mediocre work, and high-quality performance is a natural representation of how they perceive their worth. As someone said, *"We leave our fingerprints on everything we do"*;
- Perhaps the greatest benefit will come from the positive mental attitude they maintain. With such an attitude, others admire and respect them. They become people of influence and role models, inspiring others to go the extra mile as well. They are also more valuable to their employer and open the door to better career prospects and advancement.

Napoleon Hill, the author of "Think and Grow Rich", had this to say: *"The man who does more than he is paid for will soon be paid for more than he does"*, and *"Start going the extra mile, and opportunity will follow you"*.

Og Mandino, who wrote "The Greatest Salesman in the World", said: *"Always render more and better service than is expected of*

59

you, no matter what your task may be".

Choosing to apply the principles outlined will enable you to:

- Acquire the habit of self-discipline, making it easier to use it in all areas of your life; and
- Lay the foundations for living a life of significance.

They will also initiate a chain of events influencing what you manifest in your life, viz:

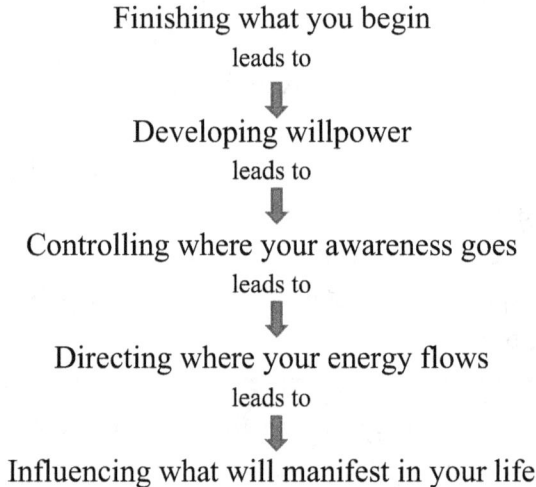

Finishing what you begin

leads to

⬇

Developing willpower

leads to

⬇

Controlling where your awareness goes

leads to

⬇

Directing where your energy flows

leads to

⬇

Influencing what will manifest in your life

Applying Self-Discipline To Everyday Tasks

Four methods may be employed to apply self-discipline to daily tasks:

- Use willpower;
- Employ affirmations;
- Apply the 5-second method;
- Make a task enjoyable.

Willpower

Forcing yourself to do what you don't feel like doing is the least productive and efficient way of applying self-control because you will experience what psychologists call cognitive dissonance. This mental conflict occurs because your feelings are not aligned with your actions. In other words, you encounter an emotional struggle to be overcome by willpower.

You may be able to exercise willpower several times, on specific occasions. Still, for most people, the mental exertion, with a feeling of discomfort, will eventually cause them to give up.

This is what happens to new year's resolutions. We resolve to go to the gym three times a week, eat healthily, etc., and start enthusiastically, only to abandon our resolutions days or weeks later. The task of forcing ourselves to act against our feelings is demanding, and consistency is hard work.

However, as difficult as it is, if we can persist in exercising willpower for a continuous period of at least 21 days, there is a fair chance that we will develop the habit of maintaining the desired action.

Affirmations

Affirmations are statements we use to keep our minds focused on taking desired actions.

For example, the sayings, 'Do it now' or, as the Nike advertisement says, 'Just do it!' are both affirmations. Whenever you are inclined to procrastinate or put off a task, say to yourself, "Do it now', and without thinking further, get into action.

An affirmation can be very effective if you remember to say it and act immediately without getting in touch with your feelings.

Say, for example, you want to get up every weekday morning at 05:00, though it is cold and dark, and choose to employ an affirmation for this purpose. You might apply the affirmation, "Just get up!". To use this declaration, you must automatically, without thinking, get up when the alarm rings. If you start contemplating how cold and comfortable it is, you are tempted to hit the snooze button and will not get up until much later.

As with willpower, affirmations are only successful if they are implemented for a sufficient time to acquire a habit, usually at least 21 days.

The 5-second Rule

Mel Robbins has developed an interesting and effective method to stop an involuntary response. She calls it the 5-Second Rule.

According to Robbins, whenever you find yourself in a situation where a negative habit is triggered, countdown from 5 to 1. In other words, stop and say to yourself: 5,4,3,2,1. This action creates the needed gap for you to choose your behaviour.

By creating a gap between your thinking and actions, you can consciously decide what to do without being pushed into an automatic and spontaneous response by your emotions.

Make a task enjoyable

The fourth technique for motivating yourself is finding ways to make an activity enjoyable.

Some time ago, I decided to exercise by doing some road running. I was not too fond of jogging but felt I needed to do so to keep in shape. Unfortunately, my resolve didn't last long. After a few days, I procrastinated and eventually stopped exercising.

One day I decided to see if I could make jogging an enjoyable experience. But what could I do to enjoy running? I thought about this and came up with a solution.

I've always loved reading and found it appealing to listen to books. So, I bought myself an MP3 player, downloaded an audiobook, and found that road running posed no problem if I could listen to something I liked.

On one occasion, I was so interested in a story that I lost track of the distance I had run. When I reached the end of the audiobook, I discovered that I was about eighteen kilometres from home and didn't want to run back without listening to something. So, I phoned my wife and asked her to fetch me.

You will never have any problem doing what you love. By finding ways of making a task enjoyable, you won't need to exercise willpower to do it. Instead, you will be eager to do what would otherwise be a chore.

The ultimate purpose of applying self-discipline is to improve the quality of your life by achieving what is important to you. By employing the strategies outlined, you will be able to exercise self-control until self-discipline becomes a habit. When that happens, you will have mastered one of the core ingredients to becoming successful.

9: BUILDING RESILIENCE AND MENTAL TOUGHNESS

The word resilience comes from an engineering term that refers to the ability of an object to bounce back and resume its normal state, like a tree that bends in the wind and returns to its normal shape after the storm subsides.

Just as a physical object requires strength and flexibility to rebound into shape, so do people require the same attributes to demonstrate resilience.

The American Psychological Association defines *mental resilience* as: *"The process of adapting well to adversity, trauma, tragedy, threats or stress"*. In other words, mental toughness is coping effectively with adversity and difficult circumstances.

A resilient and mentally tough person sees problems and challenges as part of life and believes that setbacks, complications, obstacles, and impediments must be overcome to achieve anything worthwhile.

To use a mountain climbing metaphor, the mountain is the obstacle, resilience is adapting to bad weather and other impediments, and mental toughness is the determination to reach the summit.

Although resilience and mental toughness are separated to explain their concepts, the two are inextricably linked, like the strands of a DNA molecule. They, therefore, go together.

The 4Cs Of Resilience And Mental Toughness

Professor Peter Clough and Dr John Perry developed a 4C framework that identifies the key components of mental toughness.

They are:

- Control,
- Commitment,
- Challenge, and
- Confidence.

Let's consider each of these components in turn.

Control

The dichotomy of control is a concept first introduced by Greek philosophers around 300 BCE. The basic premise is that there are some things we can control and others we cannot, and knowing the difference can greatly impact our mental stability.

Understanding that some things are beyond our capacity to control enables us to divide events and circumstances into two categories - things we can do something about and things outside our power to change.

Things under our control are those emanating from our thoughts and behaviours, such as:

- Beliefs,
- Values,
- Ideas,
- Perceptions,
- Interpretations,
- Actions,
- expressions, etc.

Everything else is outside our control, including:

- What other people say and do,
- What happens to us,
- The opinions that others have, even if they are prejudiced,
- The weather,
- The economy,
- Load-shedding,
- Corrupt politicians,
- The future, etc.

By not distinguishing what we can and cannot control, we experience inner turmoil because we:

- Try to control things over which we have no influence, and
- Do not take responsibility for things we can change. When we refuse to accept responsibility for our attitudes and actions, we become immobilised and resort to complaining, moaning, criticising, and behaving as though we are victims.

When we know what we can and can't control, we don't worry about trying to change the inevitable. We can accept what we can't change and change what we can. Epictetus, a Greek philosopher, said: *"Make the best use of what is in your power, and take the rest as it happens."*

Viktor Frankl made this statement in his book Man's Search for Meaning: *"When we are no longer able to change a situation, we are challenged to change ourselves."*

The flowchart that follows illustrates the dichotomy of control.

The Dichotomy of Control Flowchart

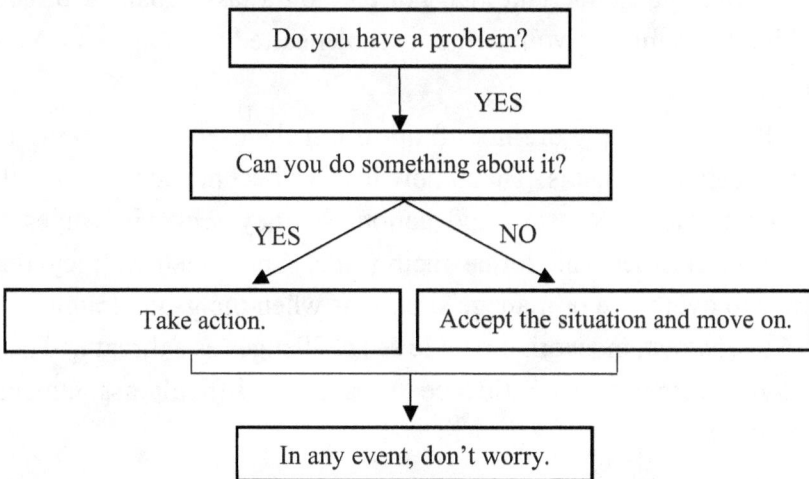

```
          ┌─────────────────────────┐
          │   Do you have a problem? │
          └────────────┬────────────┘
                       │ YES
                       ▼
       ┌──────────────────────────────┐
       │  Can you do something about it?│
       └───────────┬──────────────────┘
             YES   │   NO
          ┌────────┘   └────────┐
          ▼                     ▼
 ┌─────────────────┐  ┌───────────────────────────────┐
 │  Take action.   │  │ Accept the situation and move on.│
 └────────┬────────┘  └───────────────┬───────────────┘
          └───────────┬───────────────┘
                      ▼
          ┌──────────────────────────┐
          │ In any event, don't worry.│
          └──────────────────────────┘
```

Commitment

This is the second component of mentally tough people, differentiating the average from the exceptional. Most people are usually involved in achieving objectives and undertaking tasks. However, resilient people are more than involved. They are committed. What is the difference, you might ask?

Involvement means inclusion. It is taking part in a project, action or undertaking. However, you can be involved without being committed.

Commitment is an obligation, or pledge, to devote oneself fully to a cause. A committed manager can be relied upon to do what it takes to achieve objectives, even if it means extended effort and the denial of self-indulgent pursuits.

A committed person is never negligent and does not do things half-heartedly. Any task undertaken reflects that person's worth and is the visible embodiment of his or her work ethic.

A useful principle to adopt is always doing your best at everything you undertake. Do not take on a task, goal, or project without committing yourself to it wholeheartedly.

Challenge

Resilient people are not afraid to test themselves by taking on new, difficult projects. They know that we become competent only through effort, exposure and action, so they seek challenges to acquire, enhance and refine their skills. Consequently, they find ways to overcome or manage situations when things get tough.

In contrast, most other people see challenges as a threat and lack the motivation and confidence to take on difficult assignments voluntarily.

Confidence

Confidence describes the extent to which people feel certain of their abilities.

Those who rate highly on confidence have the resilience to overcome setbacks, and obstacles will usually stiffen their resolve.

So even after experiencing devastating circumstances, they bounce back. People who are low in confidence are easily discouraged and are inclined to give up when things get tough.

For these reasons, self-confidence is essential to resilience and mental toughness.

10: FORMING GOOD HABITS AND OVERCOMING BAD ONES

A habit is an unconscious behaviour that occurs spontaneously and frequently, without deliberate thought. Habits are estimated to govern more than 90% of our behaviours. Therefore, habits exercise considerable control over our lives, for better or worse.

William James, the father of modern psychology, wrote: *"Most daily choices may feel like the products of well-considered decision-making, but they're not. And though each habit means relatively little on its own, over time, the meals we order, what we say to our kids each night, whether we save or spend, how often we exercise, and the way we organise our thoughts and work routines have enormous impacts on our health, productivity, financial security, and happiness"*.

Since habits dominate so much of our lives, and because they occur without thinking, it is essential to form good habits otherwise, by default, we will acquire bad ones that prevent us from being happy, successful, and financially secure.

How Habits Are Formed

For many years, a study of how habits develop was the focus of The Brain and Cognitive Sciences Department (BCS) of the Massachusetts Institute of Technology (MIT) in Boston, USA.

At the BCS, neurologists surgically implanted sensors into rats to record what occurs inside their brains when given tasks perform. Scientists were particularly interested in what occurs in a section of the brain called the basal ganglia for habits to develop. This organ is the size of a golf ball, situated close to the brain stem, where the brain meets the spinal column. It controls automatic behaviours, such as blinking and swallowing. It is also activated when we are frightened or confronted with a life-threatening event. (The fight or flight response originates in this part of the brain.)

MIT researchers discovered that rats with injured basal ganglia had problems learning to do things that other rats did quite easily, such as pressing a button to release food or finding a path through a maze to reach a piece of cheese.

With new technology, scientists could implant sensors into the basal ganglia and observe what happened in the rats' heads while performing routines.

In one experiment, researchers placed the rodent into a T-shaped maze with a piece of chocolate on the left side of the T. The structure had a partition in the passage that opened with a loud click when the researcher opened it.

The following is a diagram of the maze with a rat in position:

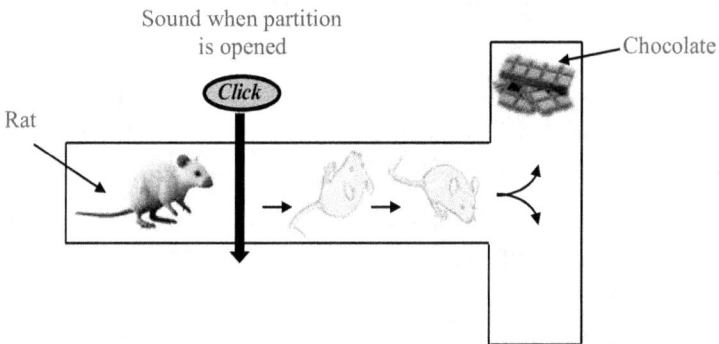

When the rat heard a click and saw the partition slide back, it would wander up and down the passage, scratching walls and sniffing the floors and sides. It could smell the chocolate but didn't know where it was. Eventually, the rat arrived at the T-junction, sniffed left and right, moved backward and forward and soon found the chocolate. While all this was happening, MIT scientists received feedback on what was happening inside the animal's brain.

While the rodent sought the chocolate, its basal ganglia worked furiously. With each action, its brain exploded with activity, analysing every scent, sound, sight, and movement. The rat was not meandering randomly. It was processing information. When the rat found the chocolate, the brain cells seemed to light up like a Christmas tree.

After a few days of exploring, a shift occurred in the brain's decision-making centre; it went quiet. All the rat had to do was remember where it had gone earlier.

About a week after that, even the decision-making centre shut down. The rat had learned where to go and didn't need to think at all. The behaviours of running forward to the T-junction, and turning left to find the chocolate, had been internalised in the basal ganglia. This organ had stored repetitive patterns of behaviour to form a habit.

An efficient brain enables us to perform acts automatically, so we no longer need to dwell on processes. We decide, and we act. This means we can do other things after an action becomes habitual. For example, a driver can listen to the radio, talk to a passenger, observe the countryside, and think of what to cook for dinner instead of concentrating on the process of driving the vehicle.

The *Habit Cycle*

After conducting hundreds of experiments, scientists discovered when and how the basal ganglia internalised habits. They called this the habit cycle. It comprises three steps:

First, there is a cue, which is the trigger that sets off the habitual response.

Second, there is a routine or behaviour.

Finally, there is the reward or pay-off. The reward tells the brain whether the routine is worth remembering and applying.

The habit cycle of the rats studied at MIT is illustrated below:

Routine

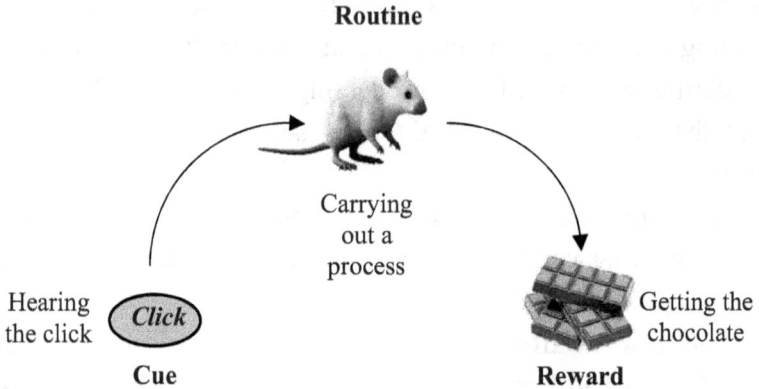

Carrying
out a
process

Hearing
the click   *Click*

Getting the
chocolate

Cue

Reward

Over time, the process creates a typical response: the cue, routine and reward are embedded in the basal ganglia as a neural circuit, and a habit is formed.

Can Habits Be Changed?

Habits never disappear completely. They are encoded in the structures of our brains and remain there. However, habits are not destiny; they can be relegated to the background or replaced.

Although past patterns remain in the brain, we can use the habit cycle to create new neurological routines to replace bad habits. After creating a replacement habit, it becomes as automatic as the previous one.

Think of it this way. Suppose you placed a tin of red paint on top of a ladder while painting a feature wall in your house. Unfortunately, you reached out too far to get into a corner and knocked the paint over. The red paint splattered all over an adjacent wall, which was beige, a colour you wanted to retain.

Now assume that you waited a few hours, then covered the splattered wall with a coat of beige paint to make it look as it was. Would the red splash still be there? Yes, it would, underneath the newly painted beige colour. But would it matter? No, because it is hidden and not seen.

So, it is with habits. We don't have to worry about erasing bad habits. Instead, we replace them with good ones, so they don't bother us anymore.

With knowledge of a habit cycle, we can install a desirable, positive response instead of an unwanted habit.

Examples Of Bad Habits

Bad habits may range from hurtful, obnoxious behaviours to biting nails and anything in-between. Any unconscious, automatic behaviour that occurs repetitively is a habit, and if it causes problems in your life, you need to replace it. But how do you do that?

In a paper called "Log Life Prescription", authors Harrar and Gordon identified several bad habits that have a debilitating effect on our quality of life. They are:
- Snacking when not hungry;
- Procrastinating;
- Eating junk foods;
- Frequently expressing anger or demonstrating impatience;
- Skipping breakfast;
- Drinking too much alcohol;
- Smoking cigarettes or electronic inhalers ;
- Over-engaging in social media;
- Overusing medication, such as tranquillizers, painkillers, sedatives, etc.

Replacing Bad Habits With Good Ones

To replace a bad habit, apply the following three steps:
1. Keep the old cue;
2. Change the routine (i.e. implement the desired habit);
3. Maintain the old reward.

These three steps constitute the golden rule of habit change commonly applied to treat alcoholism, obesity, behaviour disorders and virtually all destructive or undesirable habits.

Probably the most successful rehabilitation organisation in the world is Alcoholics Anonymous (AA). This organisation is internationally known for its outstanding work in freeing people from the devastating consequences of alcoholism, substance abuse and addictions.

AA attacks the habits that surround toxicomania. The organisation encourages its members to identify the cues that activate alcoholic habits. In part of the programme, people list everything that triggers the craving for alcohol. After that, AA asks alcoholics to establish the rewards they get from drinking.

Getting drunk is excluded because it is not a benefit. Nobody enjoys waking up with a headache, losing control, vomiting, making a fool of themselves and doing terrible things such as abusing their children and partners.

Most alcoholics will say that the benefits they derive from alcohol are that it enables them to:

- Cope with difficult circumstances,
- Escape from physical or mental pain,
- Relax,
- Find companionship in bars and among friends who also drink,
- Lose inhibitions,
- Free themselves from anxiety, fear, or guilt,
- Openly express themselves, etc.

To achieve these rewards, members have a support system. They can talk about their problems and get help and advice from others who have encountered similar issues. Addicts also regularly attend meetings for companionship and are helped to create new routines when confronted by cues. They can also contact a personal sponsor to help them through difficulties if things get bad.

The method employed by the AA ensures that triggers and pay-offs remain the same, whereas routines and behaviours change. Eventually, new behaviours are activated by old cues and existing rewards, creating an alternative habit cycle.

Some may think that addressing alcoholism is too far from their reality. So, let's take a more common example.

Suppose you wish to develop the habit of eating more healthily. You eat too much junk food because it is convenient, and you enjoy pizzas, hamburgers, chips, hot dogs, etc.

You know this food is bad for you and have tried to change, without success. To make things worse, not only have you put on weight, but a recent medical examination has revealed that you are pre-diabetic. Consequently, your doctor has strongly advised you to change your eating habits by significantly reducing your carbohydrate intake.

You ponder the cues and notice that you have several fast-food menus available to order food whenever you feel hungry. So, what do you do when it's time to eat?

The solution is to replace your routine or habitual behaviour with a healthier one. To do this, start by listing wholesome foods you like. For example, you may enjoy eating fruit, meat, nuts, salads, and so on. These can replace high-carb meals.

Next, find food outlets that deliver healthy food you can enjoy. Get their menus and order nutritious alternatives instead of going for fast foods. The reward is that you still relish your meals.

Do this long enough (at least 21 days), and you will have broken the habit of habitually consuming large amounts of carbohydrates. You may occasionally enjoy a pizza or hamburger, but you won't do so spontaneously and without thought.

The Visual Swish

Another way of changing routines is to apply a process developed by Dr Richard Bandler using a method in a type of therapy called Neuro Linguistic Programming or NLP.

The purpose of the Visual Swish is to replace unwanted behaviours (or routines) with desired behaviours. This technique programmes the brain's neural pathways to move in a different direction.

There are seven steps to a Visual Swish

- Establish the cue and reward;
- Picture the unwanted behaviours;
- Imagine the desired behaviour;
- Check for ecology;
- Set up the two pictures (unwanted and wanted behaviours) and swish (exchange) them;
- Clear your mental screen and repeat the swish several times;
- Test.

Let's explain each step in greater detail.

Step 1: Establish the cue and reward

Assume you want to stop biting your nails. You do this whenever you are nervous and stressed. Think of the most frequent cue that triggers anxiety (such as meeting a deadline etc.). Now ask yourself what nail-biting does for you. It might give you comfort, release tension etc. That is your reward.

Step 2: Picture the unwanted behaviour

The second step in applying the Visual Swish is to specify the unwanted behaviour or habit and the context in which it takes place.

In our example, biting fingernails is the unwanted behaviour, and the context is the time or place it occurs. This might be when you are anxious or have a deadline to meet. If you cannot find a single context common to all nail-biting occasions, find something you must do every time to engage your unwanted habit. For instance, bringing your fingers to your mouth.

Step 3: Picture the desired results

To carry out this step, picture the desired behaviour or outcome and imagine how you would look or behave if you had already accomplished the desired change. Keep adjusting this image until it is compelling.

Make sure that the image is a dissociated picture of yourself.

This means that you are not experiencing the change. Rather, you are observing the change from a detached perspective in your imagination.

For example, you might look at nails that are neatly clipped. In your mind's eye, you note a feeling of satisfaction and well-being with this image. There is no tension, only a sense of comfort.

Step 4: Check for ecology
Checking for ecology confirms whether you are congruent with the desired image in Step 3. As you perceive the outcome, do you have any hesitation or misgivings? Does any part of you have the slightest objection? If the answers to both questions are no, continue. If any part of you objects to the change, you must resolve your inner conflict before moving on to the next step. You do this by examining the internal discord you are feeling, and resolving it. If you cannot do this alone, you need the help of a counsellor or mental health professional.

Step 5: Set up the two pictures and swish (exchange) them
Set up both the existing image and desired image. Then begin by visualising the unwanted behaviour in front of you. Imagine, for example, biting your nails. Then place a small, dim picture of the desired image in the lower right-hand corner of your visual field. You now have two pictures in your mind, a big one where you are biting your fingernails and a small, dim one in the corner, where you are looking at a set of neatly clipped fingernails.

With the two images set up, quickly swich them by having the large, desired image in front of you while collapsing the unwanted image into the corner. In other words, one picture is being exchanged for the other, leaving you with a large, desired image (nice fingernails) in your mind and the unwanted picture, small and dim, in the corner.

Do this quickly. As fast as you can say "swish," reverse the images.

Step 6: *Clear your mental screen, set it up again and repeat the swish several times*

You clear your mental screen of the two images by opening your eyes, looking around and taking a deep breath. This is called "break-state." After doing this, set up the two images again, as described in the first part of step 5 and repeat the process. Continue doing this six or seven times.

Make sure you swish in one direction only (i.e., replacing the unwanted behaviour with the desired image) and break-state by opening your eyes and breathing deeply between each swish.

Step 7: *Test*

Test to see whether the desired self-image has taken. To do this, try to hold the picture of the unwanted behaviour and see what happens. If the Visual Swish has been effective, the desired image will immediately replace the unwanted behaviour. In other words, setting up the unwanted picture will automatically give way to the desired one rather than your former habit.

If you can keep the unwanted behaviour in mind, i.e., it does not switch to the desired image, back up and repeat the entire process.

The Visual Swish completes the habit cycle, as shown in the diagram on the next page:

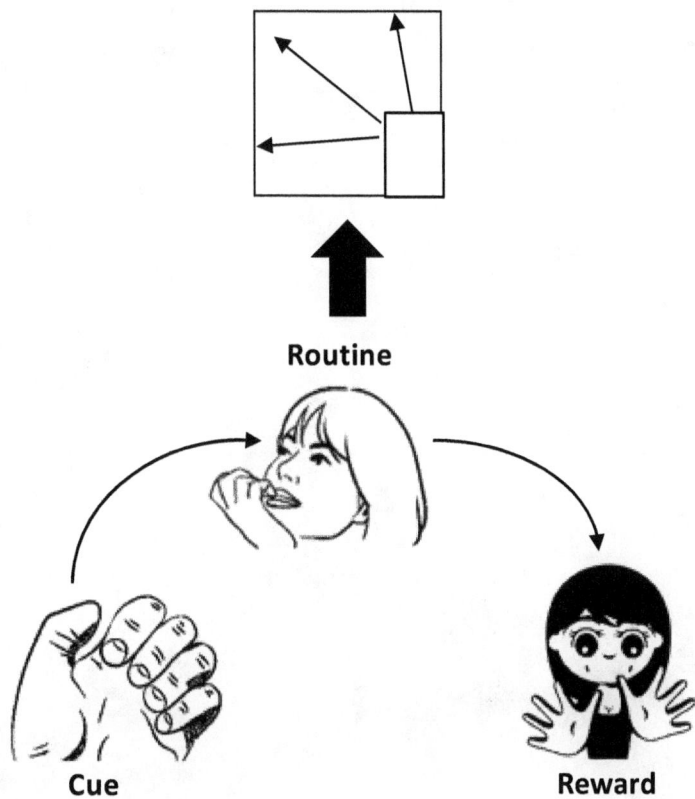

Routine

Cue

Reward

Ray Laferla

11: APPLYING RATIONAL THINKING TO MANAGE EMOTIONS

Rational thinking is one of the key attributes of emotionally intelligent people.

Whereas most people get upset by trivialities or annoying situations, the emotionally intelligent person is able to reflect on what is happening and come to a reasoned explanation to understand and find a possible solution to the dilemma. In other words, emotionally intelligent people do not allow aggravating issues to create mental disturbances. They know the cause of emotional disturbances and apply rational thinking to resolve issues.

The Cause Of Emotional Disturbances

What causes emotional disturbances and mental suffering? Does emotional distress occur due to things outside of us, such as a belligerent customer, financial difficulties, or loss of some sort, such as poor health or retrenchment? According to cognitive psychology, it's none of these things. Outside events and external circumstances have no power to upset a person.

In other words, what upsets us is how we think about something and our interpretation of the event, not the thing itself. No person or situation can make you annoyed, depressed, or even happy and confident. Each of us creates our own feelings by the nature of our thoughts.

The A-B-C of Emotions

Albert Ellis, a psychologist and originator of Rational Emotive Behaviour Therapy, has provided a simple yet powerful model for understanding why we feel the way we do.

Ellis points out that most people think that an activating event (A) causes emotional consequences or feelings (C) and that people have little or no control over the process. This is illustrated in the following diagram:

A **(Activating event)** Someone insults you	→	C **(Consequences)** You feel angry

According to Ellis, the idea that an activating event is the direct cause of an emotional disturbance is fallacious; A does not cause C. You do not, for example, get angry because someone has insulted you.

To support his theory, Ellis cites the following case:

Suppose you pass by a house. Someone on the balcony attacks you verbally, swearing and calling you nasty names. You will probably become upset and get angry at his nastiness.

Now, imagine that the house you are passing by is a psychiatric home, and you believe the person swearing at you is a patient. Would you feel upset in this instance? Probably not, because you would perceive him as crazy.

In this illustration, the activating event (A) is identical in both cases. (Swearing at you and calling you names). However, your feelings at point C (emotional consequences) differ greatly. The reason? Something happens between A and C. In the first case, your internal dialogue may have resembled something like: "How can he call me those names? I won't stand for it".

In the second instance, you may have said to yourself: "Shame. He's sick. It's not his fault, and he can't help it." With this kind of self-talk, one will likely feel pity and even compassion, but not anger.

Therefore, we can conclude that something between (A) and (C) is the real cause of emotional disturbances. Albert Ellis says that the belief (B), or interpretation about (A), causes (C). If this belief is irrational, the consequence is to become emotionally disturbed. In other words, people get upset because they think upsetting, irrational thoughts, not because of events and what others say and do.

The A-B-C of emotions is, therefore:

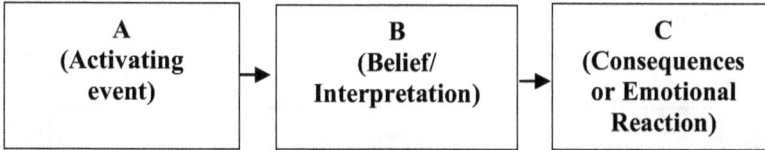

A (Activating event)	B (Belief/ Interpretation)	C (Consequences or Emotional Reaction)

Let's take another example. Suppose a sixty-year-old man was put on early retirement after being employed by his company for twenty-five years. His feelings about this event are likely to be negative and upsetting. What kind of thinking accompanies emotional disturbances? These are listed under B, with the resulting feeling under C.

A (Activating event)
- They forced me into retirement.

B (Beliefs or thoughts)
- This is a disaster.
- The company has no right to do this to me after 25 years.
- I can't afford to retire, and I'll never get another job at my age.
- I gave my company the best years of my life then they do this terrible thing to me!
- I'm too old to start again.
- I'm useless.

C (Consequential emotions)
- Anger, resentment, bitterness, depression, anxiety, etc.
- The feelings under C are examples of dysfunctional beliefs and judgements, otherwise known as irrational thinking.

The Turnaround Method For Eliminating Emotional Disturbances

The turnaround method comprises three steps that empower a person to consider the situation rationally and turn around an irrational conclusion (which is the cause of most emotional disturbances).

The three steps are:

Step 1 Get in touch with your feelings, label them, and identify the thoughts that make you feel bad.
Step 2 Change or dispute those thoughts by questioning their validity.
Step 3 Turn around the false belief or assumption.

What follows are a few scenarios of how irrational thinking may be disputed or challenged and subsequently turned around.

Scenario 1

A	B	C	D
Activating event	Irrational belief and thought	Consequence or reaction (emotion) arising from (B)	Disputing or challenging the irrational belief/thought
You have failed to accomplish a task satisfactorily and are criticised.	"I make so many mistakes: I'm useless."	Feelings of worthlessness and depression.	"Is it true that I'm completely useless just because I've messed up this job? Of course not!" "There are so many things I've successfully done in the past, such as …"

= Turn-around

Scenario 2

A	B	C	D
Activating event	**Irrational belief and thought**	**Consequence or reaction (emotion) arising from (B)**	**Disputing or challenging the irrational belief/thought**
At an office cocktail party, your partner made a remark that raises the ire of some of your colleagues.	"He shouldn't have said that. It's terrible!"	Feelings of embarrassment and anger.	"Must my partner always share my opinions? Of course not! He has a right to think differently."
			I cannot take responsibility for what my partner says or how others react. Those are his choices."

= Turn-around

Scenario 3

A	B	C	D
Activating event	Irrational belief and thought	Consequence or reaction (emotion) arising from (B)	Disputing or challenging the irrational belief/ thought
Several friends have asked you to go drinking with them, and you don't want to.	"I've got to go drinking with them, even though I don't want to."	Feelings of being pressured and of helpless.	"Do I always have to do what my friends want? What would happen if I didn't go drinking with them tonight?
			Probably nothing. But if I lose their friendship because of their demands, they are not genuine friends, and I'm better off without them."

= Turn-around

To illustrate the workings of the three-step Turnaround Method, I have reproduced a transcript of a counselling session between myself and a client (with my client's permission). As you progress through the narrative, notice how each step flows into the other, providing a natural and seamless progression that leads to awareness, insight and, eventually, freedom from emotional distress.

The story began when a fifty-five-year-old client was placed on early retirement to make way for an affirmative action appointee. At the time, he was the Senior General Manager, Operations of a large organisation that was a leader in its field.

My client joined the company shortly after completing his university degree at the age of twenty-four. For thirty-one years, he served the company devotedly, often at the expense of his family.

Quickly he climbed the corporate ladder of success and, at the relatively young age of fifty, was appointed Senior General Manager, a position second only to the Managing Director. Now, five years later, he was given his marching orders.

My client's forced early retirement came as a complete surprise and shock. Rather than being given the chop, he expected to be appointed Managing Director in the next year or two since the current MD was approaching sixty-five.

I need to emphasise that money was never a problem. The company was willing to boost my client's pension fund so that his monthly income would continue at about 85% of his retirement salary, with annual increases to match the inflation rate. Furthermore, my client had invested wisely over the years and was a wealthy man in his own right. With this background, the following counselling session took place:

Client: *"So, there it is. Because of the government's affirmative action policy, I've been kicked out of my job. In the new South Africa, being white is almost as bad as being black under the apartheid government. Then, they called it Job Reservation, now they call it Affirmative Action and BEE (Black Economic Equity)."*

RL: *"So, how do you feel? Be specific."*

Client: *"I feel rejected, violated and very angry that I am a victim of blatant racism dressed up as political correctness."*

RL: *"You feel rejected and angry because your company placed you on early retirement. You've also told me that money is no problem. So, why are you distressed?"*

Client: *"Why? Because I gave the best years of my life to the company, and they just threw me out as if I was a nobody. They discarded me. They rejected me after all I've done for them. How would you feel if it happened to you?"*

RL: *"So, you think that because you worked hard and conscientiously for 31 years, the company had no right to place you on early retirement? They owed it to you to keep you on board and even appoint you MD later on."*

Client: *"Damn right! I worked for that position and deserved it.*

RL: *Think about what you are saying for a moment. Is it really true that the company owes you permanent employment and that you have the right to demand the position of MD?"*

Client: *(Pause) "It sounds different when you put it like that."*

RL: *"Is what I said different from what you think."*

Client: *(Pause) "I suppose not."*

RL: *"So, answer my questions. Does the company owe you permanent employment, and do you have the right to demand a promotion to MD?"*

Client: *(Smiles) "Of course not."*

RL: *"So, both those assumptions are false?"*

Client: *"I suppose so. In the past, I've even told others that the company doesn't owe anybody anything. They work, and they get paid for their work. But there's something else."*

RL: *"What's that?"*

Client: *"They owe it to me to be fair. I've given them more than most. I've given this company the best years of my life. I've denied myself and even put the company before my family. Surely that counts for something. They could have consulted me and discussed options, but they didn't. They just threw me out like I was a nobody."*

RL: *"Is it true that you're a nobody?"*

Client: *(Angrily) Of course not!*

RL: *"And management indeed had to consult you before placing you on early retirement?"*

Client: *"Legally, they should have."*

RL: *"So, what are you going to do about it?"*

Client: *"What can I do about it? They offered to boost my pension fund substantially, and if I take the matter to the CCMA, they might withdraw this offer."*

RL: *"So, in what way did the company act unfairly?"*

Client: *"By not discussing it with me first."*

RL: *"What difference would it have made if they had discussed it with you before placing you on early retirement?"*

Client: *"Nothing. The decision was taken."*

RL: *"Let's summarise. You felt rejected and angry because the company placed you on early retirement without consultation. You think they treated you as a nobody, yet they generously boosted your pension fund. Is that right?"*

Client: *(Doesn't say anything.)*

RL:	*"What's so unfair about that? And why shouldn't the company look after its interests? They have retired you, but they haven't been unjust to you other than perhaps by discussing it with you first."*
Client:	*"You're right. If it had to happen, I wanted to be a part of the decision.*
	(Pause.) Actually, now that I think of it, maybe it's for the better."
RL:	*"How so?"*
Client:	*"Corporate politics has gotten to me in the last few years. The backbiting, people fighting amongst themselves, inexperienced people being put into high positions because of the colour of their skins and so on."*
RL:	*"And now?"*
Client:	*"Now I don't have to take that s**t!"*
RL:	*"Let's turn around your initial thoughts. Instead of you being the victim of injustice ...."*
Client:	*(Interruption) "...the company wanted a black person to do my job, and they acknowledged my service by funding my pension to place me on early retirement."*
RL:	*"How does that thought make you feel?"*
Client:	*"I actually feel OK, relieved. I guess I was overreacting. The truth is that I don't need the company and am free to live my life the way I want to. (Pause) Thank you!"*

In this case, notice that Step 2 involved asking many questions to reveal the irrationality of my client's thinking. To get to the root cause of a disturbance, we must vigorously challenge false assumptions.

Although it is relatively straightforward for a trained counsellor to apply the three-step process with a client, don't assume that a counsellor is always necessary. Anyone can use the technique on himself or herself.

If you feel bad, systematically challenge your assumptions until you reach the turnaround. Going through the process forces you to acknowledge false beliefs and interpretations, and soon you will notice a significant improvement.

I'd go so far as to say that if you don't feel relieved after having gone through the three steps, you either haven't done the process properly or are unable to be objective about the situation.

When you take responsibility for your emotional well-being and position yourself to take charge of your life, others will no longer victimise you or make you feel bad. It's all in how you think.

However, there is one caveat. In a very small percentage of cases, feeling depressed and out of sorts is not a psychological disturbance arising from faulty reasoning and assumptions. Hormonal and chemical imbalances in the body cause some conditions. These are called endogenous disturbances.

Usually (but not always), the difference between an endogenous disturbance and a psychological one is that an event or series of events triggers the latter. In biologically caused disturbances, there are typically no specific events directly associated with feelings of pervasive anxiety, depression, etc. In these cases, the perturbation is generalised and widespread.

In cases where the cause of the emotional disturbance is anything other than faulty judgements and assumptions, you should consult a medical practitioner to check whether there is a physical component to it.

12: ENGAGING FORGIVENESS TO ACHIEVE EMOTIONAL FREEDOM

Stephan Rigally was considered an excellent manager who rated high on the Emotional Intelligence scale. Over many years he led an outstanding team, excelling in productivity and always achieving their objectives, often exceeding them. Stephen had a master's degree in Occupational Psychology and understood the motivations and mindsets of his people.

One of the things that Stephen often told his staff was that, in life, many things would make them angry, and many people would disappoint them. Some may even try to hurt and injure them. However, despite these occurrences, they must never harbour resentment, anger or bitterness as these feelings will cause more damage to their souls than any misdeed, and the damage would be self-inflicted. Stephen believed that it is imperative to forgive others for any wrongdoing, no matter how bad.

Then one day, Stephen's philosophy of forgiveness was tested. His mother was murdered during a carjacking when she resisted getting out of her car. Eventually, police found the felon, who was taken into custody and charged. Stephen was informed of the day the murderer was to appear in court on multiple charges of homicide, including Stephen's mother.

Initially, Stephen did not want to attend proceedings, but he changed his mind a few days before the trial. The case had brought up repressed anger and hostility, and he wanted to see the man who killed his mother.

The day came, and the trial began. When the police led the accused into court, the defendant smiled and didn't seem to care about the seriousness of the matter. Stephen was surprised but noticed that he didn't feel angry. After staring at the accused for a while, Stephen felt sorry for the murderer and thought about what a terrible life he must have lived and how tormented he must feel below the facade he was presenting. Or worse, did the defendant kill innocent victims without feeling guilty? Was he immune to any pain he caused, and did he regret his actions? If not, he was a murderous psychopath, the inhuman embodiment of a vile person who would probably spend the rest of his life in prison.

Then Stephen put into practice what he had told his people at work. During the court proceedings, he mentally forgave the accused of murdering his mother and wished him well. With that, he left the court light of heart and feeling good.

Several months later, Stephen heard that his mother's murderer had been found guilty and sentenced to life imprisonment. Stephen thought he would be happy now that justice was served, but he felt neither glad nor sad. He had truly forgiven the man and had no desire for revenge.

Stephen's staff were surprised that their manager could forgive so easily. He was a genuine role model who walked his talk, and they respected him all the more.

Many people think forgiveness is condoning or overlooking the actions of those who have perpetrated wrongs. To think this way is to misinterpret the meaning of forgiveness, justifying the reason to hold on to feelings such as anger, bitterness, resentment, and the desire to take revenge.

In Stephen's case, he could not overlook the actions of the murderer; the mother he loved was no longer alive, and he would have to live with that. However, Stephen was free of the choke of negative emotions, and released from the pain that bound him to the murderer.

The Meaning Of Forgiveness

It is important to know what forgiveness is and what it is not.

Let's begin with what it is not.

Forgiveness is not about excusing a wrong. Those who intentionally hurt, harm, or abuse others must take the consequences for their behaviours.

Forgiveness is not about reconciliation. We can forgive without reconciling or maintaining contact with the person we release.

We do not have to tolerate offensive behaviour by forgiving. Bad behaviours are unacceptable, and therefore, *forgiveness is not about tolerance.*

Some people may think that forgiveness means denying any harm done. This belief is untrue because *forgiveness does not forget or pretend something did not happen.* That is denial. Whatever occurred did take place, and we need to learn from it without holding on to any pain.

If forgiveness is not any of the things mentioned, what is it?

To forgive means to "let go." It is a willingness to move beyond the hurt and pain to a deeper understanding. It does not deny wrongdoing but refuses to allow reprehensible acts to stand in the way of a new start. In an essay entitled "Forgiveness", Dan Carl puts it this way: *"Forgiveness means releasing your emotions concerning injustices you have experienced. It means releasing the self-image of being a victim of unfair treatment and deciding instead to be a person who has grown through and beyond a serious challenge to your well-being. It means ceasing to replay events in your mind in ways that recreate your trauma, pain, or fear so that your ongoing victimisation can cease."*

Catherine Ponder, author of The Prospering Power of Love", says: *"When you hold resentment towards another, you are bound to that person and constrained by an emotional link stronger than steel. Forgiveness is the only way of dissolving that link to get free."*

Forgiveness is, however, not only about forgiving others. It is also about forgiving yourself for any wrongs you have committed.

Ultimately, forgiveness is a gift you give to yourself. It is releasing yourself from the damaging and corrosive effects of mental, physical, and spiritual suffering.

Four Reasons To Forgive
We need to forgive to:
- Ensure peace of mind,
- Remain physically well,
- Experience spiritual well-being, and
- Maintain healthy relationships.

1. Peace Of Mind
Non-forgiveness is perhaps the most important cause of debilitating negative emotions such as anger, bitterness, vengefulness, guilt, shame, and associated feelings. These emotions shatter peace of mind and keep one in persistent agitation and anxiety.

In the extreme, feelings of rage, vengefulness, and the like lead to murder and suicide. These are the severe actions from those consumed with intense negative feelings towards others or oneself.

People who refuse to forgive live in the past. They hold on to hurt and pain as though it's a precious mantle to be preserved. In so doing, they re-experience wrongdoings repeatedly and remain bound to an issue long after it occurred.

Unwillingness to forgive creates emotional cripples, causing unhappiness and misery. Psychologists regard a lack of forgiveness as one of the major causes of psychological distress.

2. Physical Wellness
Numerous studies have demonstrated a direct relationship between emotions and health.

In breakthrough research (documented in her book "Molecules of Emotion"), Dr Candice Pert found that strong emotions release hormones called neuropeptides in the human body. These neuropeptides enter the bloodstream and lock onto the receptor cells of certain organs. Therefore, body parts store emotions, which, if negative, will ultimately incapacitate one's physical well-being.

An unforgiving spirit is devastating because it keeps one in an unrelieved state of turmoil, with emotional hurt and pain triggered repeatedly. Again and again, more negative emotions are stored in the body until a point is reached where organs become overloaded, requiring medical intervention.

Medical interventions, however, often deal with symptoms rather than causes (which may include an unforgiving spirit).

There have been many studies that confirm the direct relationship between negative emotions and physical ailments. To name just one, a study published in the American Journal of Cardiology in August 1992 found a direct unhealthy change in heart function brought on by anger. The authors found that hostile individuals were five times more likely to die at an early age than their peers, who had learned to deal with anger by forgiving others and themselves.

3. Spiritual Wellbeing

Forgiveness is one of the very cornerstones of spiritual wellbeing. Every major religion has, at its core, the doctrine of forgiveness.

4. Relationships

Lack of forgiveness destroys relationships. We all make mistakes and are guilty of misconduct. Forgiveness allows us to let go of the past, begin anew and reconnect with one another in a spirit of harmony and love.

Six Steps To Forgiveness

There are six steps to forgiveness, namely:
- Prepare to forgive;
- Specify what you need to forgive;
- Acknowledge feelings of hurt, anger, guilt, etc.;

- Where appropriate, recognise any part that you may have played;
- Learn from the experience; and
- Let go.

Let's examine each of these in turn.

Step 1: Prepare to forgive

Because forgiveness is consciously chosen, each person must be ready to release themselves from the burden of holding on to hurtful feelings.

To create the conditions for readiness, understand what forgiveness is and is not. Then recognise that you are harming yourself mentally, physically and spiritually by refusing to let go of the past. Do not expect to know why things occurred. Accept that what happened is history, and decide to move on.

Step 2: Specify what you need to forgive

Draw two lists, each specifying wrongs to forgive:
  i.   Things you have done (or not done) for which you need to forgive yourself; and
  ii.   Things others have done (or not done) that you need to forgive.

Step 3: Acknowledge your feelings

This step requires you to get in touch with your feelings. Are you experiencing anger, bitterness, frustration, resentment, vengefulness, hate, guilt, fear, shame, or other negative emotions? Write down your feelings, bearing in mind that many emotions may be linked to a single event.

Step 4: Recognise the part you may have played

People often shift blame to avoid taking responsibility for their actions. This step requires us to examine our actions and face our inadequacies. Consider the following example.

Some time ago, a senior executive named Frank was passed over for promotion after having been with his company for 23 years.

At 58 years of age, Frank felt that he needed to move up the corporate ladder to enhance his pension, which would accrue when he turned 65. When this didn't happen, he was consumed by rage and anger and spent the next three years taking every opportunity to criticise and condemn his former employer rather than make himself more valuable to the company.

Only after Frank experienced a heart attack did he face himself and admit that he had gotten lazy and failed to add value to his employer; this laid the foundation for mental and physical healing.

Note, however, that while it is important to admit our faults and take responsibility for our actions, there are times when we are genuine victims. Examples are women who are targets of rape, battered children, and those who suffer traumatic incidents such as terrorism, hijackings, etc. Such people are not responsible for their tragic occurrences.

It is crucial to differentiate between things for which we must take some responsibility and those events that were not, in any way, caused by our behaviours.

Step 5: Learn from the experience

With the benefit of hindsight, consider what you can learn from the experience. How can the incident make you a wiser, more mature, better person?

No matter how traumatic or painful the event has been, you can usually derive some benefit from it. Perhaps it has made you more understanding and compassionate, or maybe you discovered something about yourself. The experience may have led you in a different direction that turned out to be beneficial. You might even have needed the encounter to teach you something, etc.

Step 6: Let go and forgive

Having ascertained what you can learn and how you can benefit from your experience, the event has served its purpose. There is no longer any reason to hold on to negative feelings, so consciously and deliberately release them.

The next thing to do is to summarise steps 2 to 6 in writing. For example, you might say:

"I forgive .... (yourself or the name of the person) for having .... (describe the deed). From this experience, I have learned ....(say what you have learned). I am now ready to release my feelings of .... (name the negative feelings), knowing that they no longer serve me. I am wiser and more understanding for my experience, and I let go with gratitude."

With this note, you can now forgive yourself or anyone involved. The best way to do this is to perform a ritual to give forgiveness tangible expression. You can do this by burning each note and scattering the ashes. Alternatively, you may want to flush the paper down the toilet or bury it in the garden, signifying that the matter is dead. You may even wish to create a special ritual symbolising the release process.

Having freed yourself from the pain of hurtful experiences, be aware of its effects. Perhaps you feel lighter and more joyful. Maybe you feel a burden taken off your shoulders. Whatever it is, notice how much better you feel and get on with your life without the affliction of sustained negative emotions due to an unforgiving spirit.

RAISING EMOTIONAL INTELLIGENCE

The Third Domain of EQ:
Social Awareness

Ray Laferla

RAISING EMOTIONAL INTELLIGENCE

Social-Awareness

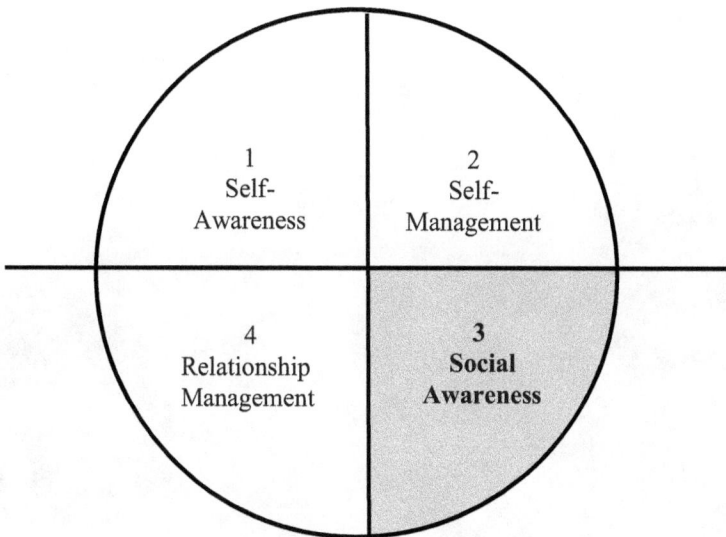

Social-Awareness contains three elements:
- Practising empathy;
- Being non-judgmental; and
- Transmuting the emotions of others.

Ray Laferla

13: PRACTISING EMPATHY

Empathy is "The ability to be aware of, understand, and vicariously experience the feelings, thoughts and experiences of others" (Webster's Dictionary).

To practice empathy, we need to progress through three stages:

- Focus attention on body language, gestures, movements and postures expressed by the other person;
- Establish rapport to connect with people;
- Master the art of attentive listening.

Body Language

The ability to discern a person's attitude by interpreting body language and behaviour is part of us. It was the primal way of communicating before we learned to speak and is, of course, how babies understand what parents and siblings are saying.

Today, the emphasis is usually on the verbal expression of thoughts, e.g., how to construct speeches and make presentations. This is relevant and appropriate since most people regard speech as their primary mode of communication.

Yet, in evolutionary terms, speech is a relatively new phenomenon corresponding to our brain's development. Until the modern era, body language and sounds (such as grunts, signs, and other noises from the throat) were the main forms of emotional expressions used to convey feelings.

All this means that most of us have shifted our attention from body language to what is being said by words expressed. All is well if these words are congruent with the speaker's genuine feelings and thoughts. However, the spoken word often hides devious intentions.

This occurs, for example, when a conman endeavours to take advantage of someone, a salesperson tries to manipulate a prospect, an unscrupulous man seeks to seduce an innocent victim, a politician lies to cover up wrongs, etc. Under these circumstances, the words spoken will be incongruent with physiology because *body language is a more accurate and unconscious reflection of what a person is experiencing internally.*

So, what a person says may be staged and fraudulent, but what someone reveals through body language more accurately represents what is felt and thought.

Facial Expressions

Facial expressions, voice, and gestures are important indicators of emotional states.

Emotionally intelligent people are able to read nonverbal expressions to establish the most appropriate way of addressing issues. If, for example, a staff member is feeling depressed, it's not wise for a manager to ask him to entertain an important client in her absence.

When interpreting facial expressions, we must consider the context in which they appear. Also, the extent of expression will reveal the depth of feelings.

Sensory Acuity is the term psychologists use to scan a face to establish internal representations and their meaning. To develop sensory activity, you need to focus on facial features with particular reference to the following:

- forehead (e.g., frowning, lined);
- eyebrows (e.g., drawn together, arched);
- eyes (e.g., staring, closed);
- mouth (e.g., smiling, scowling);
- position of the head (e.g., tilted, head back);
- chin (e.g., jutting out, raised);
- colour of skin (e.g., blushing, pale).

Establishing Rapport

Building rapport is essential for showing empathy. It is also a key factor in managing relationships to make people feel comfortable and at ease.

This subject is covered in Chapter 16 of this book.

Active Listening

The ability to listen attentively is one of the most valuable, skills for a person to master. Emotionally intelligent people know that listening is critical to building productive relationships.

Bad listening habits are the root of most misunderstandings and communication failures. The next five characterisations are often the root of poor listening habits.

The Faker

All the outward signs are there: nodding, making eye contact and giving the occasional uh-huh. However, the faker isn't concentrating on the speaker; his mind is elsewhere.

The Interrupter

The interrupter doesn't allow the speaker to finish and doesn't ask clarifying questions or seek more information. He's too anxious to express his thoughts with little interest in the speaker's words.

The Intellectual Listener

This person tries to fit the speaker's words into a theoretical construct or paradigm. He is not tuned in to the speaker's perspective, nor does he seek to uncover the underlying feelings or emotions attached to the message.

The Rebuttal Specialist

This individual only listens long enough to form a rebuttal. Her point is to use the speaker's words against him. At worst, she is argumentative and wants to prove others wrong. At best, the rebutter intends to make the speaker see another point of view.

The Advice Giver

Giving advice can sometimes be helpful. However, at other times, it interferes with communication because it does not allow the speaker to articulate feelings or thoughts fully, and doesn't help the speaker solve his own problems.

A much better way of helping people is to ask questions and encourage them to find solutions. Offering suggestions, or giving advice, is suitable only if the speaker doesn't know what to do and seeks counsel.

The Four Strategies Of Active Listening

Active Listening engages the listener to understand the real meaning of what is said. We achieve this by allowing the speaker to talk freely, whilst acknowledging and affirming understanding of the message in a supportive and non-intrusive manner.

The four strategies of Active Listening are:

1. Ask Questions

The purpose of asking questions is to confirm understanding.
There are essentially two types of questions:
- Clarifying ('Do you mean ...?' 'Can you give me an example?');
- Explaining ('So tell me why...?');

2. Reflect To Confirm Feelings

Effective listeners understand the speaker's feelings and not just words. To do this, they use words beginning with "you felt" or "you feel." For example: "You felt belittled and angry" or "By not having been invited to the meeting, you feel marginalised and unappreciated."

Sometimes a reflected feeling is inaccurate. In this instance, the speaker will usually correct the inaccuracy by saying something like, "No, I didn't feel belittled. I felt disrespected and angry."

3. Paraphrase

To paraphrase is to restate the speaker's message in different words. The purpose of paraphrasing is to ensure that the message is correctly interpreted.

4. Summarise

An active listener summarises from time to time to:
- review what is discussed,
- pull together major points,
- prepare the ground for further discussion.

Ray Laferla

112

14: BEING NON-JUDGMENTAL

The Universal Dictionary defines judgement as: "Criticism or condemnation passed by one person on another." When we judge others, we criticise or condemn them.

Non-judgement refers to someone who does not categorise people as good or bad or situations as right or wrong. The person who practices non-judgement is mindful that a lot lies beneath the surface that we are unaware of. If we knew why people behave as they do, we would be far less likely to criticise or condemn them.

We may not agree with behaviours that hurt or offend, but we can try to understand why people behave the way they do. Instead of being critical, try to find causes and reasons. Rather than condemning a person, an emotionally intelligent person thinks: "That behaviour is appalling. I wonder why he acts that way?"

Why Do We Judge?

Humans like putting things into boxes of right and wrong to simplify life.

The labels we place on people provide a frame of reference for our beliefs and behaviours. Consequently, our moral decisions are based on our judgements because we believe in their validity and correctness.

Forming judgements, then, serves the ego. We decide what behaviours are acceptable and feel we have the moral right to condemn others who think and behave differently.

The Consequences Of Judging Others

Judgements can be very detrimental to our thinking and our

relationships. Why? Because after labelling and categorising people negatively, we tend to:

- become critical,
- feel superior to those we condemn,
- stop relating, and listening, to others,
- defend our beliefs irrationally
- become negative and perpetuate stereotypes,
- cause others to judge us in return,
- create conditions of conflict,
- close our minds to different values and beliefs,
- become estranged, and are avoided, by those we judge,
- destroy our well-being and happiness.

The Benefits Of A Non-Judgmental Attitude

A non-judgmental attitude will benefit you, your family, friends and companions. These benefits include:

- **Improved relationships.**

   You create an atmosphere of acceptance when you approach others with an open, non-judgmental attitude. This makes people feel comfortable in your presence, and they will like you;

- **Greater empathy and compassion.**

   People will share their views, feelings and experiences with you when you have a receptive, non-critical approach. When they do so, it makes it possible for you to comprehend their perspectives, giving you a greater understanding of their conditions and enabling you to empathise with them with compassion.

   An event that illustrates this point occurred when Sarah, a manager, was given a specialist to assist her team on an important new project.

   Sarah was a stern, authoritarian go-getter with a strong inclination to exercise tight control. Danny, her assigned team member, was a computer expert who expected to be allowed to exercise his professional skills without interference. He was a private, introverted person who appeared aloof and preferred to work alone.

Sarah and Danny shared an immediate dislike for one another, and she judged him to be an uncooperative person with few social skills, a huge chip on his shoulder, and a poor team player.

One day, a colleague told Sarah that Danny had recently experienced the death of his wife and child in a shooting incident at a convenience store. This news touched Sarah as she had lost a daughter less than a year before. In her case, the cause was cancer.

Several days after she learned of Danny's traumatic incident, Sarah had an opportunity to talk with him, so she asked him about the death of his family.

At first, Danny refused to talk about it. However, Sarah told him she understood his grief because she had also lost a child. They ended up having a conversation during which Danny mentioned that over the last two years, he had endured extreme traumas such as financial distress due to a misplaced investment, the loss of a brother (who committed suicide), a home invasion where he, his wife and daughter, were in the house locked in a bedroom while the burglars ransacked their house. Danny finally succumbed to depression and was only now learning to cope emotionally with what had happened in his life.

These revelations helped Sarah to see Danny differently, and she began to understand why he appeared aloof; he was still in grief and coping with depression.

Over the next few weeks, while Sarah and Danny continued to work together on their project, Sarah tried not to judge him and understand what he was going through.

She realised that Danny's behaviour was not a reflection of his attitude or personality but rather the result of the difficulties and challenges he was coping with.

In the months that followed, Sarah found that her attitude shifted. She was no longer critical of Danny and supported him where she could. She also realised that Danny's experience taught her there were reasons why people acted the way they did. Consequently, Sarah was less inclined to judge and began to feel more connected with her staff.

This example shows that a non-judgemental attitude can create space for empathy and compassion and that people are more nuanced and complex than appears on the surface. By getting to know people, we understand them better, and with understanding comes acceptance, not judgment;

- **Enhanced self-awareness.**

Taking a non-judgmental attitude helps you become more aware of your own shortcomings with the realisation that we all have weaknesses. Accepting this fact, and not being critical of it, makes you more open-minded towards yourself and others.

We must remember that nobody is perfect, and relationships will be difficult and fragile without tolerance and acceptance of weaknesses;

- **Greater open-mindedness.**

Being non-judgmental also helps you be more receptive to novel ideas and experiences. Untethered to preconceived notions or fixed ideas, you are more likely to embrace possibilities and view new situations with curiosity and openness.

How To Become Less Judgmental

To become less judgmental, become aware of how negative you may be. Notice yourself criticising or condemning others, and how frequently you do so.

Remember that few things are fully good or bad; it all depends on your perception of things and how much information you have. So, get facts, observe, and be open to divergent views, opinions, and behaviours. Ask questions, discover divergent perspectives, and understand why people do what they do. Don't put labels of good or bad onto people. Rather contemplate reasons and possibilities as your awareness increases.

Bear in mind that non-judgement does not mean you have to agree with what others say or do. It's alright to have a different viewpoint and to think differently. Realise that it's acceptable for people to be whoever they are, just as it's fine for you to be who you are. It is possible to care for people even when disagreeing with their values, beliefs, and actions.

Discovering the experiences and values of others is an important part of practising non-judgment. Ask questions, listen, and you will find that behind every façade is pain, heartache, hurt, grief, distress or anguish, and everybody sits beside their own pool of tears. If we are prepared to dig deep and get in touch with what others have encountered, how they have suffered, and how their experiences have shaped their beliefs and perceptions, we will find that they are no different to who we are.

John Bradford, an English Reformer, who watched people go to the execution chamber for their crimes, said, *"There, but for the grace God go I."*

To become less judgmental and more accepting, avoid putting people into categories. Refrain from labelling people and situations based on your biases and assumptions. Instead, accept differences without attaching value judgments.

If you find this difficult to do:

    i.   Get in touch with your negative feeling and name it. Let it come up, be aware of what it is, and stay with it for a while. Relinquish any effort to modify it.

    ii.   Having gotten in touch with your feeling, notice if you have any guilt or fear about it. Negative feelings are often associated with guilt. They also emerge in response to fear or anxiety.

          Psychiatrist David R Dawkins says that fear is related to survival and that whenever we feel threatened, survival behaviours automatically kick in to protect ourselves. We do this by verbally attacking with criticism and condemnation, sometimes even getting physical.

          If you experience guilt or fear, question yourself, and ask why these perturbations exist. If they are irrational, question the validity of your perceptions and beliefs. (For more details about this, refer to Chapter 11).

    iii.   After embracing the negative feeling and questioning its validity, surrender it. Let it go and move on.

15: HELPING OTHERS DEAL WITH THEIR EMOTIONS

Helping others deal with their emotions means applying strategies to improve four of the primary emotions described by Paul Ekman. I have already addressed these in the context of understanding emotions (Chapter 3). However, in this chapter, the focus is on helping others to deal with specific emotions that may handicap them, namely:

- Sadness;
- Fear;
- Anger; and
- Disgust.

Helping Others Transmute Emotions

Before applying a particular strategy, it is important to know what the other person feels and how intense those feelings are. You might want to ask questions and prompt individuals if they cannot label their emotions.

It also helps to know how the other person perceives you. Are you a friend, a bystander, or are you associated with the cause of a grievance? The strategy you employ will need to consider your connection with that person.

Also, observe non-verbal factors such as tone and voice volume, facial expression, posture and other cues. If, at any time, appearances indicate that you are not calming or improving the situation, either stop your intervention or change your strategy.

With these factors in mind, let us now consider how we may transmute the emotions of others regarding sadness, fear, anger and disgust.

Sadness

The way to interact with unhappy people is to listen to them and display empathy.

Never minimise their circumstances or criticise them overtly or covertly. To tell a depressed woman that she must snap out of it, or a man that he is overreacting, is insensitive and demeaning.

Often, just by taking an interest, being patient, and listening, troubled individuals will come to terms with their problems on their own.

If appropriate, use touch in a way that communicates understanding and support. A touch on her shoulder, or your hand on his arm, is a strong signal of connection. It clearly reveals that you care about the person and empathise with him or her.

Sometimes it is helpful to provide suggests on how to resolve an issue. When emotionally entrenched in a problem, we often cannot evaluate the situation rationally and need a confidante to help us find a solution from a detached perspective.

A good tactic for lessening sadness is to encourage the individual to keep busy and engage in meaningful activities. With nothing to do, idly sitting by will likely make the person focus on mistakes, misfortunes, and unhappy predicaments.

Bear in mind that sometimes sadness has biological or endogenous causes. If so, it may be temporary, such as pre-menstrual dysphoric disorder, usually occurring in women about two weeks before menstruation. In other cases, depression may require medical intervention requiring the services of a medical practitioner or psychiatrist.

Fear

Fear ranges from anxiety to phobic responses and terror. Therefore, the strategies you use to help others cope will depend on the intensity of the behaviour expressed. There is, however, a basic process for dealing with fear.

First, assess the severity of the fear and how it affects the individual. If the person is experiencing anxiety, you may want to provide the person with information or assistance that puts the matter into perspective and minimises the perceived threat.

Say, for example, a friend is worried about making an important speech, you might want to go through the presentation with him, providing advice and reassurance.

Also, offer comfort by explaining that speaking anxiety is normal. Practically every presenter is concerned about the talk not going well, the audience responding unfavourably, creating a bad image, and so on. Public speakers rate this dread as the top fear they have.

Speakers should, therefore, be encouraged to accept fear as normal. They should use it as a stimulant for giving the best possible speech by preparing as thoroughly as possible and applying proven practices, such as:

- Structuring the presentation in an effective manner,
- Doing deep breathing exercises before the presentation,
- Displaying positive body postures (confident walk and stance, smile, and smooth, open gestures),
- Delivering the presentation in a confident, pleasant tone of voice, which is neither too soft nor too loud,
- Remembering to pause at strategic points,
- Using illustrations and examples, etc.

If you are endeavouring to help someone overcome the fear of public speaking, and you have never made a presentation yourself, you might want to surf the net to obtain information and discuss various strategies with your friend or colleague. This action is particularly helpful as it shows that you care and are committed to that person's welfare.

The concept of providing reassurance, information, and discussing ways of dealing with matters, applies to all types of fear.

Fear can be described by the acronym **FEAR**: False Evidence

Appearing **R**eal.

The evolutionary purpose of fear is to protect us from harm, injury or loss, and we are moved to action to protect or defend ourselves by fearing adverse consequences. For example, if you are studying for a degree and fear failure, you may be motivated to study more to assuage that fear. Similarly, fearing heights may cause you to attach a secure fastener to yourself when working on the roof to replace tiles. Or the fear of contracting AIDS makes you unwilling to engage in casual, unprotected sex.

Therefore, fear is an effective motivator intended to lead to constructive action.

However, fear becomes dysfunctional when it immobilises people or causes inappropriate avoidance behaviours. This may occur when, for instance, a woman refuses to open herself to a new relationship after the traumatic end of a previous one. Or when a man refuses to take on a new challenge for fear of failing.

Many fears cripple people emotionally, and the common denominator of these inappropriate states is that they prevent action. They stop or block us from dealing with the problem, so we either freeze or flee from constructive engagements. And the reason this occurs is that we imagine the worst possible outcome.

However, imagined conditions exist only in the mind and are not real. Mark Twain said, *"I've had a lot of worries in my life, most of which never happened."*

When we imagine bad things happening, it is natural to fear them. But fear is usually irrational. So, we overcome fear by gathering information and doing something about it. That is why Twain also said, *"Do the thing you fear, and death of fear is certain."*

Returning to the acronym, **F**alse **E**vidence **A**ppearing **R**eal, you can help others overcome their fears by providing valid and reliable information about the anticipated harm or hurt they imagine and encouraging them to take appropriate action, with your support.

Anger

Anger is a normal human emotion that occurs whenever we experience abuse and neglect or are belittled and exploited. It can range from mild annoyance to intense rage and is sometimes appropriate.

Appropriate anger never targets an individual; it focuses on what was said or done and does not shame, belittle or judge. So if, for example, an office worker fails to follow instructions and causes severe problems, it would be proper for her manager to get angry and inform her of the consequences of neglect. It might even be fitting to take disciplinary action, depending on the severity of the issue.

In this case, anger drives the manager to take suitable action. However, at no time should the manager, in his agitated state, shout or defame the woman, calling her names and saying that she is incompetent or useless. If he is emotionally intelligent, he acknowledges his anger and focuses on resolving the problem, ensuring it does not happen again.

If the manager cannot control his rage and lashes out at his subordinate, especially if this is a typical response, he may have anger issues.

Leigh McInnis, Executive Director of Newport Healthcare, says: *"Having anger issues usually means that someone has trouble regulating or communicating their anger and often acts out destructively, potentially harming others or themselves."*

How, then, does one help someone with anger issues?

First, anger issues are complex; unless you are a trained therapist, you should not attempt to deal with an entrenched behaviour pattern. The thing to do is to encourage the individual to seek professional help.

However, do not endeavour to help when the aggressor is agitated. He or she will interpret your intervention as criticism and is likely to become even more enraged.

Remember that it takes at least twenty minutes for a human nervous system to regulate itself and return to normal levels, as long as you don't repeatedly bring up the incident. So give yourself at least an hour before addressing issues accompanied by emotions of anger. If, after that time, strong feelings have not subsided, delay dealing with the issue until there is a measure of composure.

If the person is seething and outraged, acknowledge his feelings and give the person space. Stay calm and let the individual know you are willing to talk and help address the problem when he has calmed down.

The time to encourage the person to seek help is when the individual is in a receptive frame of mind, and you can discuss the matter calmly. For instance, in an office situation, a suitable occasion would be during a performance appraisal or review. With friends and family, it may be appropriate to bring up the matter when you are discussing personal growth or relationship issues.

When discussing the issue, avoid making judgemental statements such as, "Stop being so dramatic", "Why are you overreacting? It's no big deal", or "What's the matter with you?"

An important factor in dealing with a person with anger issues is never to criticise and be judgmental. Your position must always be to help and not to try and force change.

Disgust

Disgust is a feeling of distaste or strong disapproval aroused by something offensive or insulting. For example, if a speaker says something blatantly racist, it may be appropriate for people in the audience to walk out in disgust.

However, sometimes people perceive specific behaviours as unacceptable, not because they are offensive in themselves, but because they have strong beliefs about right and wrong. For example, some parents believe they should never spank their children, while others believe corporal punishment is needed to correct deviant behaviour.

Disgust can also arise because of prejudice, bigotry, discrimination, or beliefs and perspectives opposed to accepted norms.

An example occurred after the South African government changed the law in 2006 to legally permit same-sex marriages. Soon after, the state legislated that marriage officers were not allowed to show discrimination and were required, by law, to conduct these marriages, whether or not they agreed with them.

Shortly after the government promulgated the law, many Christian ministers resisted being forced to marry gay people. These ministers said they were against the new law because same-sex unions were unnatural and went against biblical injunctions and their Christian values.

Soon after, ministers were given only two choices: either conduct all types of marriages or have their licences withdrawn. Needless to say, they were disgusted, and disapproved of this ruling. Consequently, many pastors resigned from their ministries in protest.

We need to know that a feeling of disgust can be valid or irrational based on one's perspective. In the latter case, it is not for us to judge people: we may not agree with them, but it is inappropriate to condemn others for their views.

There are four things we can do to help people who experience disgust.

i. Listen actively

It's important to allow people to express their feelings, knowing they will not be judged or criticised. Do not interrupt with comments like, "You are exaggerating" or "Don't take it personally." Simply listen and try to understand the other person's view. Remember that you don't have to agree with people's opinions, but you do need to respect them.

ii. Acknowledge emotions

Let people know that whatever they feel is all right and that disgust is normal if they feel that cherished values are discarded. Acknowledge their emotions and, if you support their perspectives, say so. If not, try to understand where they come from.

iii. If the disgust is inappropriate, or extreme, try to broaden peoples' outlook

Inappropriate disgust is an everyday experience to something perceived as revolting. For example, while dining, the subject of unusual meals came up. One guest said that he ate goat meat for the first time while visiting an African country, which tasted surprisingly good. This disgusted several people; one lady even said she felt like puking at the thought.

If it is appropriate to correct misconceptions, you might want to ask questions and discuss the matter to identify the source of the disgust. In the case of the lady revolted by the thought of eating goat meat, an ensuing discussion made her realise that she believed goats were dirty scavengers that consumed all types of dirty and horrible things. A local farmer quickly challenged her ideas by providing information that corrected her false perceptions. Later, while she still did not want to eat goat meat, she no longer reacted to the thought of it.

iv. Offer help by providing resources

If someone is experiencing persistent feelings of disgust, or struggling with specific issues, it might be helpful to direct them to resources such as books, counselling or support groups.

Let's say, for instance, that a friend tells you that her marriage is failing because she does not see sex as a healthy, desirable part of her life. Because of her upbringing, she perceives intimacy as disgusting and necessary only for procreation. In this case, it would be appropriate to suggest that the lady seek professional help, and encourage her to see a sex therapist or suitably qualified counsellor.

Remember that everyone experiences emotions differently and reacts uniquely to life events. Therefore, there is no formula for helping someone who feels disgusted. The most important thing is not to judge the individual. Instead, provide support and assistance in a way that shows you care.

Ray Laferla

RAISING EMOTIONAL INTELLIGENCE

The Fourth Domain of EQ: Relationship Management

RAISING EMOTIONAL INTELLIGENCE
Relationship Management

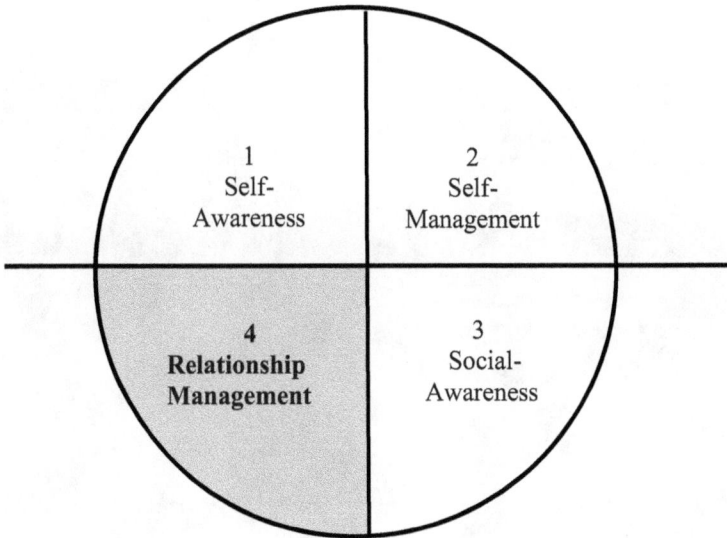

In the chapters that follow, we will address three key aspects of managing relationships:
-   Influencing and persuading people;
-   Managing conflict;
-   Dealing with difficult individuals.

Ray Laferla

16: INFLUENCING AND PERSUADING PEOPLE

Emotionally intelligent people know that, for better or worse, we always influence others, and others affect us. The question is whether we are connecting with people in a way that is positive and beneficial to all parties.

Robert Cialdini, a social psychologist, has written a book entitled, "Influence: The Psychology of Persuasion", in which he describes several principles pertinent to the subject of influence. These principles cover a range of factors described in this chapter.

Also, different combinations of these principles will apply in specific instances, with some being more relevant than others. What they have in common is that they automatically trigger decisions for people to respond positively, and provide support, without thinking about it.

Decision Triggers

We live in a world where we have a great deal of information. Data is readily provided through the media, the internet, publications, and other sources that add to, and often contradict, existing knowledge.

The sheer volume of facts and data is so large that no one can take in all the information on any subject; there is just too much. The result is "information overload."

So, how do people make effective decisions if nobody can absorb and process the full range of knowledge available on any topic? By resorting to shortcuts. People pick what they consider key issues, or core factors, and respond to them. These core factors are called "decision triggers."

What are these decision triggers? They are the seven principles of influence, namely:

1. Rapport;
2. Sequencing;
3. Reciprocity;
4. Uniqueness;
5. Authority;
6. Affection; and
7. Agreement.

Context And Attitude

Undergirding and supporting the seven principles are two factors that need careful attention: the context of the interaction, and the attitude expressed.

Context

The context is the environment or situation in which people find themselves. For example, if a saleslady has just five minutes to see a potential client, the context would be very different than if the client gives her an hour.

Let's also assume you see a customer who has had a bad experience with your company's products or services. This context would be much more disadvantageous than one where the customer was delighted with past encounters.

Influencing a person in an uncomfortable context (e.g., too hot, cold, noisy, when the person is tired etc.) is far less advantageous than in a comfortable or pleasant context. Therefore, we must create the best environment to interact positively with others.

Attitude

Our attitudes influence everything we say and do. For better or worse, attitudes significantly affect the outcome of personal interactions. Good attitudes create good results, and bad attitudes lead to poor outcomes.

A good attitude is considerate of the other person, is not

judgmental, and seeks to advance the well-being of another.

A bad attitude is taking advantage of others or influencing them for personal gain without regard for their welfare.

Having explained context and attitude, we are ready to move to the seven principles of influence and persuasion.

The Seven Principles Of Influence And Persuasion

Principle # 1: Building Rapport

The Oxford Dictionary defines rapport as "a relationship marked by harmony, conformity, accord and emotional affinity."

To the extent that we are in agreement or aligned with another person, both verbally and nonverbally, we are in a state of rapport. To achieve this, we may need to pace the other person.

Pacing

Pacing means matching other people's:
- Dress code,
- Body language,
- Speech patterns (rate of speech, tone, volume etc.),
- Words and images, and
- Breathing.

When we are "in sync" with another person, we experience their thoughts and feelings. By doing so, we also naturally express ourselves in the same or similar body language.

Just as body language expresses thinking and feeling, so can it influence these modalities. So, if you want to align yourself with another person, pace the other individual by reflecting the same or similar body language and way of speaking.

However, be careful not to mimic and copy the other person so it's obvious. This would be interpreted as making fun of the individual and is likely to be resented. Instead, be subtle and natural so that it's not noticeable.

Leading

Whereas "pacing" is behaving in ways similar to another person, leading influences the other person to do something different.

To lead, first pace. Then, when you feel there is rapport between the two of you, make a small change in your posture, tone of voice, breathing etc. If the other person follows, this confirms that a rapport exists between you.

The chart on the next page illustrates the flow of activities that occurs in the process of pacing and leading.

The Flow of Pacing and Leading

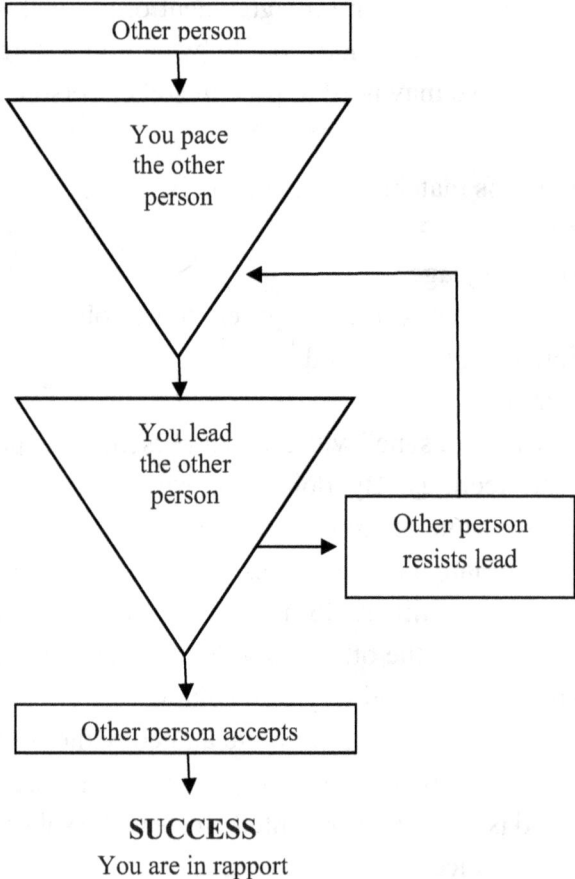

Principle # 2: Sequencing

The Universal Dictionary defines a sequence as the *"following of one thing after another."*

Ordinarily, the sequence in which we place things suggests a rank order, so #1 is usually bigger, better, or more important than #2.

Because rank order is part of how we see things, we naturally link situations or events with others that proceed or follow them. Seldom, if ever, do we isolate or separate things that appear in the same context.

Because of our associations between objects, acquisitions can appear cheap or expensive, and better or worse than they are. Therefore, proper sequencing can make a difference if used effectively.

The Contrast Axiom

This axiom says, "If we present two or more items after one another, and the second is substantially different from the first, we will compare the second item with the first."

To illustrate the Contrast Axiom, consider the letter (on the following page) received by the parents of a 19-year-old girl named Mary, who had completed her matric and proceeded to work for one year as a UN volunteer.

The context for Mary doing voluntary work was that she wanted to be independent of her family after finishing school. She was Greek, and it was customary for single girls to stay with their parents until they married. Also, Mary's father was demanding and domineering. He laid down the law, and when Mary said she wanted to do volunteer work for the UN, her father forbade it.

Nevertheless, Mary persisted to the chagrin of her dad and was selected to go to northern Kenya for a year to distribute food parcels and minister to the poor and sick in East Africa.

Mary's father was furious. He refused to speak to her and told her she must not ask him for help unless she was prepared to come home.

About ten months later, Mary's parents received the following letter:

Dear Mom and Dad,

I haven't written to you for a long time because so many things have happened, and so quickly, I just couldn't get around to it. Things have settled a bit so, at last, I'm putting pen to paper.

Please sit down. I have a lot to tell you, which isn't all good news. So don't continue reading this letter until you are seated. Ready? O.K., let's go on.

First, I need to tell you that I was involved in a bad motor car accident. Two of my colleagues were killed, and I was in a coma for two weeks with a broken sternum and serious internal injuries. Fortunately, I pulled through. Except for an occasional blackout, and some difficulty breathing, I'm fine.

I survived, thanks to a young black Kenyan man who lives in a tribal village not far from where the accident occurred. He took me to his settlement, and a traditional medicine man attended to my injuries.

When I came round from my coma, this witchdoctor gave me the most horrible muti I've ever had. Even now, when I think about it, I want to vomit. Yet I am addicted to the stuff. It's a dagga-based concoction that I must have, to relieve me of pain. Anyway, I guess it's better to be an addict than die.

While in the village, I got pretty lonely, so something developed between me and the guy who saved me – Joseph is his name.

Although Joseph is relatively uneducated (he only passed grade 5), he is a good man. He cared and looked after me; I couldn't have survived without him. As soon as I was well enough, we became lovers.

Why am I telling you this? Because I've just discovered that I'm pregnant. Please don't be cross with me. I want to have this child, whether or not Joseph and I eventually marry.

There is one other thing I need to tell you. Joseph has just been told that he is HIV positive. I went for tests yesterday and will get the results in the next few days. Even if I have HIV, I've been informed that there is a good chance my baby will be OK. So, you can look forward to being grandparents to a healthy child.

Now that I have updated you with what has happened, I need to tell you that I was not involved in a car accident, I was never in a coma, I am not a drug addict, there is no Joseph, and there is no possibility that I am HIV positive because I am not sexually active.

However, I have run out of funds and need $100 urgently. I know I promised not to ask you for money, but I really need it, and I wanted you to see this request in its proper perspective.

I love you and am longing to see you again. Just another two months, and I'll be home.

Your loving daughter,
Mary

The Contrast Axiom, the central tenet in the Sequencing Principle, influences people to take specific action based on a distinctive or idiosyncratic perception.

In Mary's case, by first outlining a terrible situation, she followed it up by saying it was all untrue, but she needed money. At that point, her father was so relieved that his daughter was safe and well, that he willingly sent her the money. He probably would not have done so if Mary had asked him outright.

Salespeople often use Contrast Principle to persuade customers to buy expensive items.

How is this done? Remember that "expensive" is a relative concept. Something is expensive when compared with a cheaper item. So, instead of allowing a potential customer to compare a product or service with something cheaper, salespeople deliberately present a more expensive option first, knowing that the prospect will reject it. Then, when this happens, the salesman comes up with another product or service that is more affordable. Even though the second purchase may still be expensive, it will appear inexpensive compared to the first option.

Guidelines for applying the Principle of Sequencing

➢ Create a clear context so that your offer solves a problem or provides added value. This is done by identifying and clarifying a problem and then providing a solution – in that order.

➢ If cost is an issue, pair a product or service with more expensive items so that it appears to be cheap by comparison.

Principle # 3: Reciprocity

The Principle of Reciprocity states that people feel obligated to return favours.

When we give something to someone, we create a feeling of debt or obligation in that person. It is natural for anyone who has received favours to want to do something in return to repay the debt, to cancel the obligation.

Therefore, if you accept a dinner invitation from a friend, you will most likely want to invite that friend to dinner sometime in the future. This is reciprocity.

Dennis Regan, a professor at Cornell University, conducted an experiment in 1971 to explore the concept of reciprocity in social behaviour. It is called the Coca-Cola experiment and involved 48 students who, unbeknown to them, were paired with Regan's assistant, Joe.

At any one time, the participant and Joe would enter the gallery to rate a group of paintings. During the rating, Joe would leave the room for about two minutes. When he returned, Joe would come back with nothing or two bottles of Coca-Cola, one for himself and the other with the participant. In other words, participants were placed into two groups: one received a soda, and the other got nothing.

Shortly afterwards, Joe asked participants if they would purchase raffle tickets from him for a fundraising project. The study found that participants who received a Coke bought an average of 1,84 tickets, while those not given a Coke purchased an average of 0,60 tickets. The percentage of those who took a raffle ticket was 48%, compared with 16% for participants who did not receive a Coke.

This finding confirms that gestures of kindness can influence people's behaviour and create an obligation to reciprocate.

Guidelines for applying the Principle of Reciprocity
> ➤ Go out of your way to help people, beyond their expectations;
> ➤ Give people things they want or desire;
> ➤ If you are a salesperson, give prospective customers greater concessions or benefits than your competitors.

When applying the rules of reciprocity, implement them unconditionally. Although a feeling of indebtedness is created, it must never be imposed, enforced or expected.

Principle # 4: Uniqueness
The Principle of Uniqueness says that people desire things that are unique or difficult to obtain.

Scarce things are invariably more expensive than plentiful ones; they are also of greater value.

Psychologically, people want what they can't have. Financially, people are prepared to pay more, and emotionally they desire something with greater intensity if something is rare or relatively unobtainable.

There are essentially two motivators for action: people act because they desire something, and people act because they fear losing something. Of these two, fear is usually the stronger motivator.

People of influence harness the power of desire by highlighting the benefits of an idea, product, or service. They

- highlight unique features, and
- point out what people stand to lose if they don't accept the offer.

I knew a man named Max who was madly in love with a woman and had been dating her for more than four years. Her name was Daphne. She was also in love with Max but unwilling to commit to marriage. There were several reasons for her reluctance, two of which were;

i. Daphne's parents had a terrible marriage and, though they did not divorce, remained together under very unpleasant and acrimonious circumstances. This unhappy union placed a horrendous burden on Daphne and her two siblings, and she was scared the same would happen to her;

ii. Daphne had two other relationships in the past, both of which ended badly, leaving her highly distressed and emotionally traumatised. In both instances, her partners betrayed her, leading her to believe that she could not trust men to be faithful.

Max knew these facts but did not know how to convince Daphne to trust him. Eventually, he decided on a bold course of action. Max brought a beautiful diamond ring with him, took Daphne to a spectacular dinner and show, and afterwards proposed to her. However, he imposed conditions and followed this sequence:

- Max showed Daphne the engagement ring, saying this was the last time he would propose. If she refused him, he would leave her;
- He then said that he had saved a deposit for a house and, if she said yes, could look for suitable accommodation whenever she wanted. This would give Daphne a home of her own;
- Max also told Daphne that he was not her father, nor was he an unfaithful suitor. He had never cheated on her or anyone else, and would never do so. Instead, he would love and cherish her for the rest of his life.
- Max then pointed out that if Daphne was not happy with him, she would not be content with anyone else, given that she said she loved him. Did she want to remain single all her life, with no children or house to call home?
- Finally, Max pressed the diamond ring into her palm, held her open hand, looked into her eyes, and once more asked, "Will you marry me?" Then he waited.

For a long time, Daphne said nothing, weeping silently. Then she looked up at Max and, with tears streaming down her eyes, said a soft "yes."

Max understood the principle of Uniqueness. Daphne was given one more chance with the reassurance that what she feared would not happen. Furthermore, if Daphne refused the opportunity, she was made to realise it may not come again.

Guidelines for applying the Principle of Uniqueness.
Empathise:

> ➤ genuine scarcity;
> ➤ unique features; and
> ➤ special or exclusive information.

Principle # 5: Authority

The Principle of Authority says that people listen to and obey those in positions of authority.

As children, we all depended on authorities for survival and guidance. Parents, teachers, doctors, religious leaders, and others told us what to do and what was acceptable. Furthermore, we have become conditioned to believe that authorities have a great deal of knowledge that we need. So we unconsciously accept that experts act in our best interests.

Most adults are in awe of authority figures, and we give them the power to influence us. For this reason, people are usually willing to support and follow the suggestions of someone they regard as a legitimate authority, even if that person is actually a con artist. Such was the case with Bernie Madoff.

Madoff was a highly successful and influential person in financial circles. He owned a company called Bernard L. Madoff Investment Securities, which delivered impressive and consistent returns for his clients.

However, this was an illusion. Madoff actually ran a Ponzi Scheme; he used money from new investors to pay interest and withdrawals rather than investing funds in the Stock Market as claimed.

Madoff developed his reputation as an authority by being a prominent figure on Wall Street since the 1960s. He served as Chairman of the NASDAQ, the world's first electronic stock market and the second-largest stock exchange after New York.

Madoff was extremely well-connected and had cultivated relationships with powerful people, including wealthy individuals, influential leaders, politicians and celebrities. He was also a prominent Jewish community member supporting several major charities.

Madoff used his reputation as a highly successful investor to build trust, communicating that only he could provide consistently high returns that no one else could match. Overall, Madoff used his authority and experience to delude people through a combination of secrecy, connections, trust, reputation and professional charisma.

Unfortunately, these attributes permitted him to perpetrate one of the largest frauds in financial history.

The scheme run by Madoff unravelled in the financial crisis of 2008 when a flood of investors tried to withdraw their funds, and Bernie could not pay them. Madoff confessed to his sons that he had been running a Ponzi scheme. This revelation disturbed them so much that they reported their father to the authorities, who investigated the matter.

Bernie Madoff had defrauded thousands of investors of an estimated 65 billion dollars. He was arrested and sentenced to 150 years in prison, where he died approximately twelve years later.

The highest authority of all is credibility. A credible authority has two qualities:

- expertise; and
- trustworthiness.

Expertise is demonstrated by finding solutions and solving problems that benefit all; a so-called win/win solution.

Trustworthy people:
- Keep promises,
- Are reliable,
- Keep confidences, and
- Are sincere and genuine.

To be trustworthy, these attributes must be observed over time.

The four rules of authority
We establish authority by applying the following rules:
i.   Act professionally (punctuality, speech, dress etc.);
ii.   Demonstrate in-depth knowledge and familiarity with your speciality;
iii. Acquire valid credentials ;
iv.   Admit and address weaknesses where they exist.

Principle # 6: Affection
The Principle of Affection states that people we like, and get on well with, naturally influence us. So, the golden rule is to make

others feel important; that is how they get to like us.

Guidelines for applying the Principle of Affection
- ➢ Don't criticise, condemn and complain.
- ➢ Be kind and offer assistance when needed
- ➢ Give honest, sincere appreciation.
- ➢ Be genuinely interested in others and be a good listener.
- ➢ Use and remember names, and
- ➢ Smile.

Giving sincere appreciation
For appreciation to be authentic, it must be:
- Timely,
- Genuine
- Specific, and
- Consistent.

Everybody wants to be loved and appreciated, and giving people sincere compliments satisfies that need. This is why appreciation creates affection; we like those who value us and make us feel important.

Principle # 7: Agreement
The Greek philosopher Socrates originated the idea that one should ask questions and get people to solve their own problems rather than provide solutions. We obtain valuable insights and knowledge by asking questions to make people think. This technique is known as the "Socratic Method."

However, what is not well known is that Socrates went beyond asking questions. He led antagonists to specific conclusions by getting a "yes" response to a series of questions. In other words, Socrates asked questions to which his opponents would have to agree. He obtained a string of "yes" responses until his adversaries came to a conclusion they would have previously rejected.

If a salesperson can get a potential client to agree repeatedly to the validity of a situation, the need for certain features, the desirability of specific benefits etc., and the product or service meet these requirements, that salesperson will find it relatively easy to get a "yes" for a sale.

Desirable behaviours from others

The Agreement Principle also states that how others behave is important, especially when there are many choices and people are uncertain about what to do.

To come to conclusions and decisions, most people find it comforting to look to others who have experienced the same situation and take on their perspectives. For example, when people buy goods or services online, many will refer to references and what others say about the product or service provider. The decision they make is likely to be based on those reviews.

Guidelines for applying the Principle of Agreement

- ➢ Use the Socratic Method to get a string of "yes" responses;
- ➢ Provide information on trends and mass movements of others;
- ➢ Show examples and evidence of others' past successes;
- ➢ Share testimonials.

Eight Additional Persuasion Tactics For Everyday Use

In addition to the seven principles of influence and persuasion, we can use eight everyday tactics to influence others.

i. *Use the word 'because' to get people to help you*

When you use the word 'because' in a sentence, you give people a reason to comply with your request.

Dr Ellen Langer, a Harvard psychologist, decided to test the effect of using the word 'because'. She divided her subjects into four groups of people and directed them to a line where others were waiting to make photocopies. Their purpose was to see whether they would be allowed to jump the queue by providing a simple reason.

The first group gave a sound reason, such as: "May I go before you because I have a deadline to meet and am late?"

The second group gave a lame reason, for example: "Can I go ahead of you because I need to make only one copy?"

The third group said something like: "Will you do me a favour and let me into the line?"

The group that gave a sound reason did best. 93% of the time, they succeeded in jumping the queue. The second group did reasonably well. They had a 68% success rate. The last group that gave no reason did the worst. In only 4% of cases, they got permission to go ahead of others.

Dr Langer concluded that no matter how valid your reasoning is, using the word 'because' can significantly improve your chances of getting a positive response.

ii. **Pause**

Pausing at the appropriate time gives what you say impact.

To get attention, be quiet for a few seconds before you make an important comment. If you want people to think about something you said, pause after your statement. Done correctly, pausing puts the right emphasis on your communication.

iii. **Use silence**

When seeking the support or agreement of others, it is important that you do not come across as pushy or demanding. Make a request, seek information or ask a question, then keep quiet and let the other person speak.

When you listen, you allow people to explain themselves and reveal their thoughts. This creates a connection that facilitates understanding and enhances rapport.

While remaining silent, it is important to maintain eye contact and nod in a natural and friendly manner. Not doing this may convey the impression that you are disinterested.

iv. *To stand out, try to be first or last*

We usually remember best what happens at the beginning or end of an event. This is why speaking professionals first capture their audience's interest and conclude their presentation with something memorable. It is also why top entertainers endeavour to begin with something impressive and keep their best performance for the show's end. Finishing on a high note is an important tactic for an audience to leave feeling good.

If you are endeavouring to conclude an important contract, and are competing with rivals, try to be the first or last to see your prospective client. This will give you a better chance of concluding the deal if your sales presentation is good.

v. *Sit next to your antagonist to reduce hostility*

If you are meeting someone who dislikes or is critical of you, sit next to that person during a meeting or in a restaurant. Close proximity will make your adversary less comfortable criticising you.

vi. *Ask for a favour or assistance*

When you ask a favour of someone, you make that person feel that they are needed and even valued. Requests

Ray Laferla

for assistance make the individual feel significant at a subconscious level.

It is essential that whatever favour you ask is reasonable and that you do not try to take advantage of the person.

vii. *Nod occasionally to get someone to agree with you*

If you want someone's approval, maintain eye contact and nod while making a request or asking a question. Your behaviour will influence the person to see things from your perspective.

However, don't overdo it. Too much nodding will be seen to be inappropriate and may come across as artificial and insincere.

viii. *Form a triangle with your eyes to end a conversation*

When in the company of someone who is continually talking, and you want to end the conversation, look at the person's one eye, then the other, and after that, the middle of the person's forehead.

Do this as long as the individual continues speaking. The person will soon feel uncomfortable and terminate the discussion.

150

17: MANAGING CONFLICT

Conflict is *"A difference of opinion, dispute or argument, on a subject matter of importance."*

From this definition, we can conclude that whenever independent thinkers come together, there will be divergent views and opinions that are likely to lead to conflict.

The issue is, therefore, not to avoid conflict but to manage or resolve it. Emotionally intelligent people understand this and will address conflict situations to come to a mutually acceptable arrangement.

Remember that unresolved or mismanaged conflict usually gets progressively worse. This is because, unless we resolve disagreements early and efficiently, people tend to dig into strongly held ideas and hold on to their positions angrily. When this occurs, a retaliatory cycle becomes evident.

The Conflict Retaliation Model

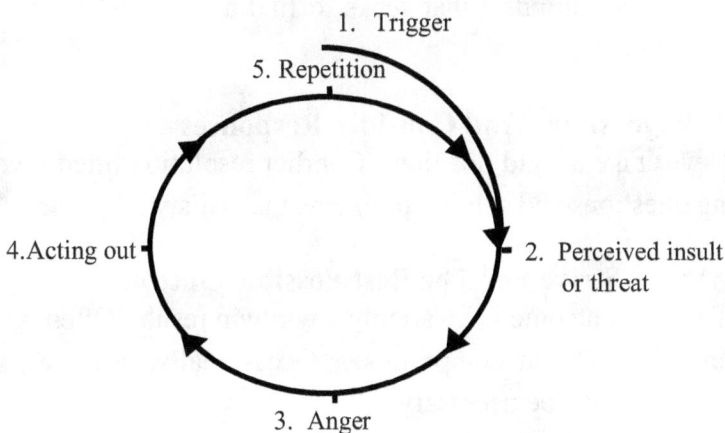

1. Trigger

5. Repetition

4. Acting out

2. Perceived insult or threat

3. Anger

Core Principles For Managing Conflict

Six principles need to be applied to situations of conflict if they are to be managed or resolved:

1. Maintain Mutual Respect

A lack of respect, or condemnation of another's position, will doom the resolution process before it even begins.

- Good questions to ask are:
- How can I discuss our differences in ways that allow the other person to retain his or her dignity?
- How can I avoid the other person feeling insignificant or put down?

2. Seek Common Ground

To find common ground explore goals, motives, and values. Try to put yourself in the other person's shoes and take particular care not to become locked into polarized positions.

3. Do Not Express Strong, Negative Emotions

Be careful not to express any criticism, and avoid negative outbursts. Any form of judgement is likely to be counter-productive, leading to defensive reactions. Instead, remain calm and rational with a mindset that seeks to find a solution to overcome diverse viewpoints.

4. Ask Questions And Consider Responses

Never take a rigid position. Conflict resolution often involves asking questions and solving problems that satisfy all parties.

5. Always Strive For The Best Possible Outcome

The best outcome is invariably a win/win result. Often, we can achieve this without compromise. Occasionally, however, some compromise may be necessary.

However, let's not think that compromise is always undesirable. Even though it may be less than perfect, reaching a mutually acceptable agreement is considerably better than not concluding any viable resolution. Compromising appropriately may, therefore, be regarded as a sort of win-win outcome because it is easier to achieve, and everybody benefits.

6. Be Open And Responsive

Hiding feelings and covering up views or actions will only lead to anxiety and mistrust. Be prepared to expose yourself and your ideas. However, when sharing a concern or a feeling about others, do so respectfully and tactfully.

Approaches To Managing Conflict

Four basic methods to address conflict issues are: submitting, compromising, forcing, and collaborating. The approach employed is usually dependent on the importance of:

- Building or sustaining good relationships and satisfying the concerns of the other party; and
- Resolving issues to the gratification of both parties.

The four basic approaches to handling conflict are shown in the following diagram:

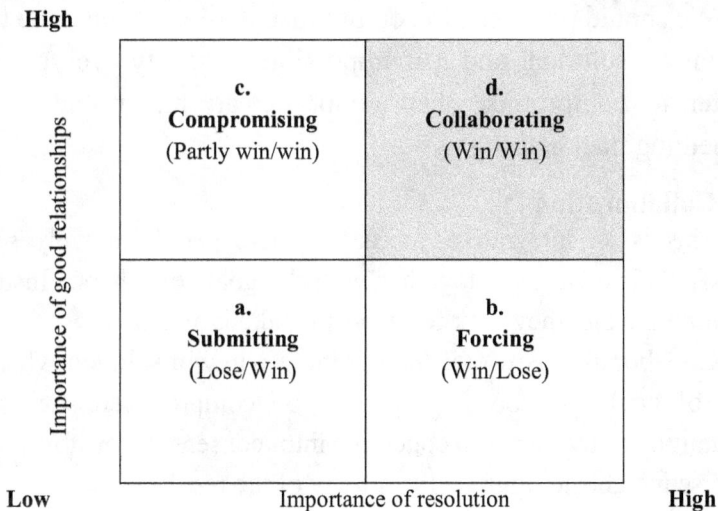

High

c. **Compromising** (Partly win/win)	**d.** **Collaborating** (Win/Win)
a. **Submitting** (Lose/Win)	**b.** **Forcing** (Win/Lose)

Importance of good relationships

Low   Importance of resolution   **High**

a. Submitting

Submitting is physically or mentally retreating from an actual or potential conflict situation. Sometimes called withdrawal, this may mean giving up or leaving the solution to fate or chance. Those employing this style do not properly address the conflict, representing a lose/win solution.

b. Forcing

Forcing is a power-oriented approach that involves threat, pressure, and intimidation to achieve objectives without concern for the needs of others.

Forcing often occurs as an open, competitive battle that produces a clear victor and a clear loser. This is rarely a productive outcome, especially if the winners must work with losers in the future. Forcing inevitability leads to anger, resistance, and resentment.

c. Compromising

Compromising is a smoothing strategy that tries to find a solution that is partly acceptable to all parties but fully satisfies no one.

We should only seek to compromise if all has been done to find a win/win solution, and it is impossible to satisfy everyone fully. Better to compromise than admit defeat: rather end up with something than nothing.

d. Collaborating

This is an integrative approach where people actively seek to satisfy their own goals together with the goals of others. Instead of splitting the pie, they look for ways to make it bigger.

Collaborating is useful for finding a win/win solution when both sets of goals are too important to be compromised, for gaining commitment by turning concerns into consensus, or for merging diverse insights to upgrade the quality of the result.

Collaborating is usually regarded as the best strategy and should be the first option for people in conflict.

There are six steps to apply when collaborating to reach an acceptable agreement. These are illustrated in the flow diagram that follows.

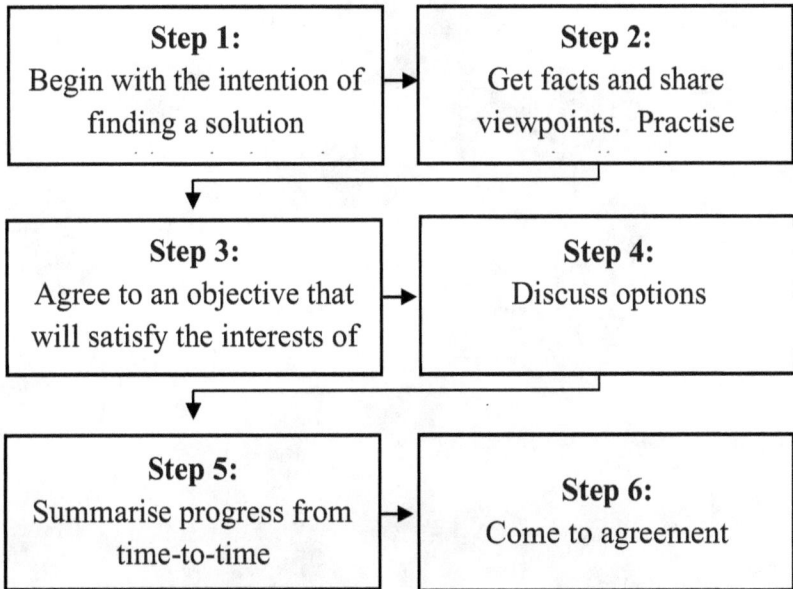

Step 1: Begin with the intention of finding a solution	**Step 2:** Get facts and share viewpoints. Practise
Step 3: Agree to an objective that will satisfy the interests of	**Step 4:** Discuss options
Step 5: Summarise progress from time-to-time	**Step 6:** Come to agreement

Ray Laferla

18: DEALING WITH DIFFICULT INDIVIDUALS

We've all been at the receiving end of insults, with nasty people throwing abuse and anger at us. No matter how much we try to reason with such people, we only irritate them more, making it a frustrating and unpleasant experience.

It is important to know that there is no way of always neutralising the tension created by some individuals. Occasionally, people may be so enraged that they block off anything we say or do, sometimes because of hidden agendas, or perhaps they are so angry or emotional that nothing gets through.

However, notwithstanding the few troublesome souls unmoved by any approach, most will respond positively to non-judgmental, friendly individuals who endeavour to help.

What follows are tactics that counsellors and emotionally intelligent people use to diffuse crises where people are belligerent and aggressive. You, too, can use these techniques with your customers, subordinates, boss, family members, and anyone else who is demanding, unreasonable and difficult.

The recommended process involves five general principles and four strategies which I call the STEP approach.

Five General Principles
Whenever we engage with difficult people, we should apply five principles in all interactions with them:

1. Don't Take Things Personally
Bad behaviour has many root causes, including frustration, stress, illness, personal issues, relationship problems and mental

distress. All of these usually have nothing to do with you. Private matters disturb and exasperate people, so they may not behave rationally. Instead, they may be inclined to project their unhappiness onto others, including you.

Of course, some obnoxious individuals are toxic by nature. They are argumentative and rebellious, with disruptive personalities that make life difficult for everyone.

So, bear in mind that, no matter the cause of problematic and abusive behaviours, they are seldom about you. People express what they feel, and you receive their emotional outbursts. For this reason, do not take things personally, thinking you are being abused and ill-treated. Rather, consider what triggered the individual to act the way he did.

If, however, you are the cause of a problem, you would be well-advised to listen to what is said and, instead of reacting, take ownership of your behaviour and make the necessary changes.

2. Listen

The natural response to a verbal attack is to defend oneself. When this happens, we become angry and don't listen to uncover the root of the problem. A typical response is, "Who do you think you are talking to?" or "I won't take this abuse from you", or "Don't raise your voice at me."

These responses are likely to infuriate the person even more, creating hostility and worsening things.

When an individual appears unpleasant and antagonistic, try to discover why the person is being difficult. Ask questions and listen. Your goal is to expose the problem to see if you can help resolve the matter.

3. Don't Judge Or Label People

To judge means to form an opinion or conclusion about something, or somebody, based on your beliefs or interpretations.

Judging people makes us label them as deficient or undesirable.

Doing so satisfies an important psychological urge: the need to justify our beliefs and opinions so that people who are different are deficient. In other words, judging and labelling others gives us a reason to feel superior and criticise others.

When people are difficult, we tend to conclude that they are uncooperative, stubborn, nasty, hostile, unpleasant, etc. These are improper labels because few people are, by nature, any of these characterisations. Our behaviours may reflect those attributes at a point in time, but they are not who we are. For example, sometimes an issue may give rise to stubbornness in defending a position, but we are not necessarily stubborn (i.e., all the time).

Similarly, you may occasionally say silly and stupid things, but you are not stupid. You make mistakes, but you are not a mistake. You respond angrily in a particular situation, but it would be wrong to label you as having a personality that can't control anger.

Judging and labelling give us a mindset to explain behaviours. But if our conclusions are incorrect, we are liable to respond inappropriately, often worsening the situation.

For instance, say that a customer strongly complains about your company's product. If you judge him as a complainer, you will brush off his grievance as trivial and either ignore him or deal with him superficially. You won't listen to ascertain why he is unhappy. Neither will you be interested in obtaining facts to address the problem. Consequently, your attitude may be a disservice to your company.

So don't judge and label people. They are not who they sometimes appear to be. Know that they are motivated to do what they do because of their experiences, feelings, and perceptions. Try to find out why they behave the way they do.

4. Be Objective, Rational And Fair

When people are objective, they are not aroused by misplaced feelings, perceptions or beliefs. Instead, they are moved by logic, rationality, and fairness.

To be objective, we must detach ourselves from our emotions, probe for reasons, and endeavour to understand. Only then can we be of help in diffusing troublesome situations.

5. Stay Calm

Never lose your cool, no matter what a person says or how abusive he may be. Speak in a quiet, relaxed manner and apologise, if necessary, even if you had nothing to do with the issue that disturbed him.

For example, you may say something like, "I'm sorry you feel that way", or "I apologise for how you have been treated." Statements such as these usually make the person feel better and less antagonistic.

The STEP Approach

With the five general principles in mind, we can move on to apply an effective strategy for handling difficult people. This strategy is called the STEP approach and comprises four actions:

- Stop whatever you are doing. Give your full attention to the person being obnoxious;
- Take a genuine interest in the person. Be sincere in wanting to resolve the situation;
- Examine the issue. Establish the problem, why it happened, who was involved, and where it happened. Ask what you can do to help resolve it;
- Proceed to solve the problem if you can. If you cannot fix the matter, refer it to someone who can, or tactfully explain why you cannot do anything about it.

www.ingramcontent.com/pod-product-compliance
Lightning Source LLC
Chambersburg PA
CBHW050125280326
41933CB00010B/1253